£1.99

£3,50

New Designs in HONITON LACE

PAT PERRYMAN AND CYNTHIA VOYSEY

Pat Perryman

&

Cynthia Voysey.

B.T. Batsford Ltd, London

ISBN 0 7134 3742 1 (cased)

Typeset by Servis Filmsetting Ltd, Manchester
and printed in Great Britain by
R.J. Acford Ltd
Chichester, Sussex
for the publishers
B.T. Batsford Ltd
4 Fitzhardinge Street
London W1H 0AH

Contents

Acknowledgment

All the patterns in this book were designed and made by us, with the exception of the following: Pattern 3 (made by Nan Steel); pattern 4 (made by Jacqueline Ford); pattern 9 (made by Ann Solman); pattern 13 (designed by Mr Stedman for the Crash Box Club of Devon and made by Tina Jackson); pattern 23 (made by Margaret Wright); patterns 24 and 25 (made by Tina Jackson); pattern 27 (designed by James White and adapted by V. Pope); patterns 34 and 40 (designed by Lee Ault and made by Tina Jackson).

We would also like to thank our families and students for the encouragement they have given us in this venture. Also our grateful thanks to Lynda Leech for typing the final draft and to Graham Ward for the photography.

Introduction

So many students over the years have asked us for our designs that we finally decided to put them together in the form of a book. The designs fall into three categories. The first section has simple flat patterns. The second has partly raised patterns and the third has all raised designs. We have purposely worked the patterns in a simple way to make them accessible to a large number of people. They can, however, be made more intricate by interpreting them in a different way.

It will be necessary to have a knowledge of Honiton lace techniques in order to make the patterns. The only instructions given are the order in which each piece is made and the number of pairs of bobbins used. The numbering of the instructions corresponds to the numbers on the diagrams. The numbers after the titles of the designs refer to the thread which was used for that particular pattern. If a different thread is used, the number of pairs of bobbins used will have to be altered accordingly.

We have also included instructions for the fillings and explanatory diagrams which should make the fillings easier to understand.

one

SIMPLE FLAT PATTERNS

1 *Wedding bells* (120)

1 Start with the right-hand bell. The clapper is worked first in half stitch, starting with six pairs and the coarse pair and increasing to ten pairs and a coarse pair. Decrease again to six pairs and the coarse at the bottom of the clapper. Cut out the coarse pair and continue in rib and leave the pairs as there is nowhere in which to sew out.

2 Sew in seven pairs and hang in a coarse pair and work the outside of the bell in whole stitch. Add one more pair, three pinholes before the corner, and cut it out three pinholes after the corner. Work around the outside of the bell, sewing into the left-hand side of the clapper.

3 Work the remaining braid section of the bell in whole stitch, with seven pairs and the coarse pair. The rib pairs left previously can now be sewn out into this section. Make the second bell in the same way.

4 Work the right-hand loop of the bow next in whole stitch, using seven pairs and a coarse pair.

5 Work the right-hand ribbon end, using eight pairs and a coarse pair. Work over the back of the loop already worked (*see Helpful Hints*, p.90).

6 The left-hand ribbon end is worked next, using eight pairs and the coarse pair. Take out one pair for the section inside the bow which is narrower.

7 Work the loop of the bow using eight pairs and the coarse pair and working over the ribbon end as on the other side.

8 and 9 The bells are filled with Brick Variation (p.94) and the underside (9) of the bells is filled with Trolly Net (p.112).

Pricking 1

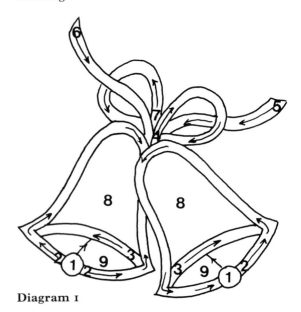

Diagram 1

Pattern 1   *Wedding bells*

2 *Tudor rose* (180)

1 Begin with the central half-stitch flower with a straight start, using eight pairs and a coarse pair and increasing to 12 pairs and a coarse pair. Weave the course thread from the outside to the inside at the intersection of each petal. Sew out. When sewing into the hole where the pairs were hung on at the beginning, do not remove the pin, but sew in beside it.

2 Work the whole-stitch petals next, using from nine pairs plus a coarse pair to 12 pairs plus a coarse pair at the widest part. Work four pin buds where indicated on the pattern. Sew out into the half-stitch flower.

3 Work the whole-stitch sepals next, starting with six pairs and a coarse pair and increasing to ten plus the coarse pair at the widest point. Make a vein down the centre by twisting the runners three times at the centre of the downrights.

Now work the fillings.

Fillings
In this instance the following were used:
a   Four pin (p.96)
b   Blossom (p.92)

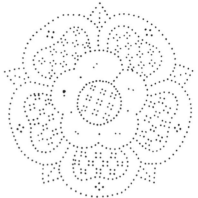

Pricking 2

Diagram 2

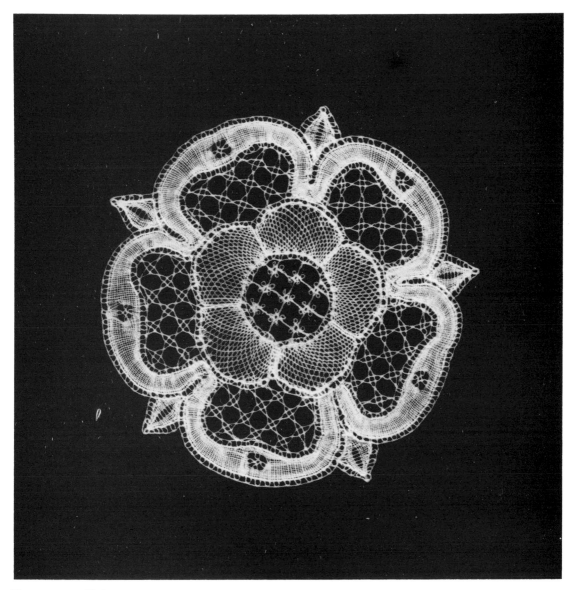

Pattern 2 *Tudor rose*

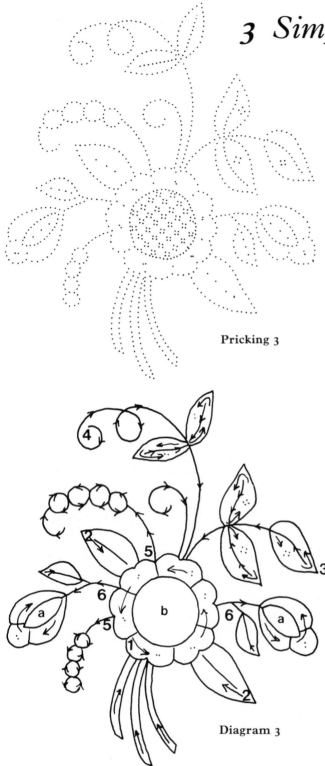

Pricking 3

Diagram 3

3 Simple flower spray (120)

1 Work the central half-stitch flower first, starting with a straight start and using nine pairs and a coarse pair. Weave the coarse thread through at the intersection of each of the petals, from outside to inside.

2 The two large leaves with a ladder trail down the centre are worked with a maximum of 13 pairs and a coarse pair.

3 Work the central rib of this leaf with six pairs, and continue in rib down the stem, finishing off on the large flower. Sew in six pairs for the whole-stitch section of this leaf and also hang in one coarse thread for the outside edge of the leaf plus one other to make a pair. Increase to ten pairs for the four pin bud. Turn at the top of the leaf with six pairs and sew into the first pin of the rib without taking out the pin. Seven pairs plus the coarse and one other will be needed for the half-stitch side of this leaf. The two side leaves are worked in a similar way, but, after working the central rib, the pairs are sewn into the stem and used for the whole-stitch section of the leaf. Turn at the top, and use to work the half-stitch side.

4 The tendril at the top of the design is worked now with six pairs. The leaves adjoining it are worked in the same way as the previous ones but with less pairs.

5 When working these tendrils it will be necessary to change the pinhole side of the rib for each section. Work up and back and, when working back, it will be necessary to sew into the rib when passing over it.

6 The buds are started at the large flower by hanging in six pairs. Rib up the stem, add a coarse pair and continue in whole stitch, using a maximum of seven pairs. Weave the coarse thread through before and after the half-stitch section. Eight pairs and a coarse pair will be needed for the half-stitch section.

Take out one pair and work the whole-stitch

14

Pattern 3 *Simple flower spray (made by Nan Steel)*

section and take out one more pair before sewing out into the first whole-stitch section. The small leaves on the bud stems were worked with six pairs and a coarse pair.

Six pairs and a coarse pair were used for the stems, starting at the tip and working up and sewing out into the large central flower.

Fillings

The fillings used were:

a   Swing Leadworks

b   Four Pin (p.96)

4 *Crescent spray* (120)

1 Work the large flower in half stitch, with a straight start. Use six pairs and a coarse pair and increase to ten pairs and a coarse pair. Weave the coarse thread through at the end of each petal from outside to inside.

2 These two leaves and their stems must be worked before the other leaves. Start at the tip of the leaf with six pairs and a coarse pair and increase to 11 and a coarse pair for the right-hand large leaf and nine pairs and the coarse for the left-hand, smaller leaf. Each of these and the other leaves on the same branch have a twisted vein down the centre. At the bottom of each leaf decrease to six pairs and the coarse pair. Cut out the coarse pair and continue to rib with the other six pairs, keeping the pinholes on the outside of the curve. (The large single leaf is worked in the same way.)

The leaves attached to these stems can now be worked.

3 The two large leaves at the base of the flower are worked half in whole stitch and half in half stitch. Start with the whole-stitch section and use ten pairs and a coarse pair, working a four pin bud where indicated; decrease to turn the top. Change to half stitch and use a maximum of seven pairs and the coarse pair at the widest point.

4 The bobbles are worked in half stitch, starting with six pairs and a coarse pair and increasing to six pairs and a coarse pair. Weave the coarse thread through at the end of each bobble. At the bottom of the last one cut out the coarse pair (having decreased to six pairs and the coarse pair) and continue in rib with six pairs, keeping the pinholes on the outside of the curve.

5 The small circles are ribbed using six pairs.

6 The filling in the large flower is Four Pin (p.96).

Pricking 4

Diagram 4

Pattern 4   *Crescent spray (made by Jacqueline Ford)*

5 *Alphabet* (120)

1 Work the flower in half stitch, using six pairs and a coarse pair.

2 Work the leaves in whole stitch. Start with six pairs and a coarse pair. Make a vein in the centre by twisting the runners twice in the middle of the downrights on each row. Increase to eight pairs and a coarse pair at the widest point.

3 Start at the bottom tip of the A with six pairs and a coarse pair, and work in whole stitch. Increase to seven pairs and a coarse pair for the widest point. Sew out into the flower.

4 Start at the bottom of the right-hand part of the A with six pairs and a coarse pair. Work in whole stitch, adding one more pair as it widens. Reduce to six pairs and the coarse pair at the end of the curl. Cut out the coarse pair and change to rib. Work to the top of the A and weave in a coarse pair. Change to whole stitch, using a maximum of seven pairs and a course pair. Sew out into the flower.

5 The bar across the centre of the A is worked next. Sew six pairs into the rib edge and sew out into the flower at the end of the bar.

All the letters are worked in a similar way.

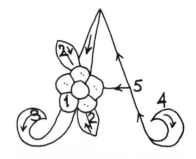

Diagram 5

Pattern 5 *Alphabet*

Pricking 5

Pricking 5

6 Spider and web (120)

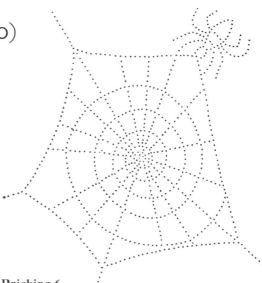

Pricking 6

Pattern 6   *Spider and web*

The whole of the web is worked in rib with six pairs of bobbins.

Start on the outside edge, where indicated, and work towards the centre and then out and finish at 1. To work the lines across the web:

start at 4 and finish at 10
start at 11 and finish at 3
start at 14 and finish at 8

Next work the spider. Start at the antennae and work them using four pairs of bobbins. Use these eight pairs for the body making 'windows' where indicated. Lay back the ends at the tip of the body. Start at 17 and work the front leg across the body using four pairs of bobbins and continue the other front leg to 7. Add two more pairs and rib across the web to 15.

Work the other lines across the web as follows:

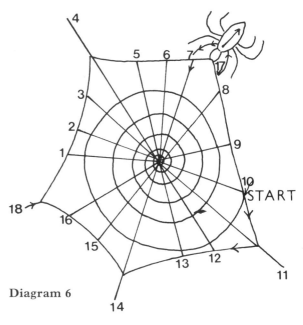

Diagram 6

start at 5 and finish at 13
start at 6 and finish at 12
start at 9 and finisht at 16
start at 2 and finish at the centre

21

7 Paisley design (120)

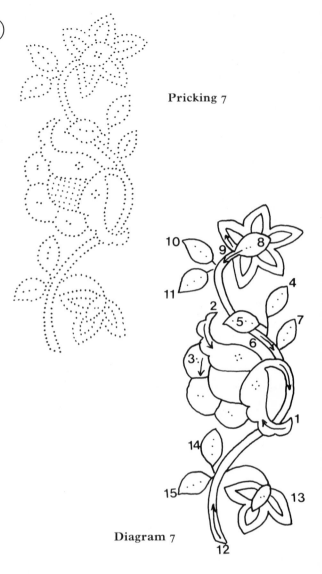

Pricking 7

Diagram 7

Start at 1 with six pairs of bobbins and a coarse pair. Increase to 11 pairs plus the coarse pair at the widest part for the four pin bud. Decrease to six pairs plus the coarse pair for the stem which is sewn out into the side of the petal.

Start at 2 and work this petal in the same way as the previous one and sew out the pairs into petal 1.

Work the scalloped part of the flowers next, using seven pairs of bobbins plus the coarse pair. Make pearls on the outside edge and weave the coarse thread through between the scallops, from outside to inside and back.

Make leaf 4 next. Start with six pairs plus the coarse pair and increase to eight pairs plus the coarse pair, twisting the runners in the centre of the downrights to make the vein. Decrease as the leaf narrows, and at the bottom have six pairs plus the coarse pair. Cut the coarse pair out now and proceed in rib with the remaining six pairs. Leave these pairs to one side at the bottom of the stem.

Make leaf 5 in the same way and sew out into the stem of leaf 4. Sew six pairs into leaf 5 to make stem 6. Also hang in a coarse pair and make the stem in whole stitch, sewing out into the flower stem. Now sew out the bobbins left at the end of leaf 4.

Start the top bud at 8 with six pairs of bobbins plus the coarse pair, and work in half stitch, increasing to eight pairs plus the coarse pair at the widest part. Decrease to six pairs plus the coarse pair for the stem, change to whole stitch and sew out into leaf 5.

Start at 9, hang in six pairs plus the coarse pair and work the outer edge of the bud in whole stitch and sew out into the stem.

Leaves 10 and 11 can now be made with the same number of bobbins as leaf 4. Start at the tip of the stem 12, with six pairs plus a coarse pair, and work in whole stitch and sew out into petal 1.

The lower bud 13 is worked in the same way as the top bud, but only increase to seven pairs for the centre half stitch.

Leaves 14 and 15 can now be made in the same way as the previous leaves.

Fillings
Suggested fillings for the large flower are:
Pin and a Stitch (p.102)
Swing and a Pin (p.106)
Diamond (p.95)

Pattern 7   *Paisley design*

8 *Heart and scallop veil edging* (120)

1 The two flowers are worked first in half stitch. Make a straight start with six pairs and a coarse pair and increase to eight pairs and a coarse pair. Weave the coarse thread through from outside to inside at the end of each petal (except the last one where you sew out into the start).

2 Sew in seven pairs along the petal of the flower. Hang in a coarse pair and work the heart in whole stitch.

3 Start the leaves with six pairs and a coarse pair and increase to ten pairs and the coarse pair. Twist the runners to make the veins down the centre.

4 Work the whole-stitch section of the scallops next, in the direction indicated. Use six pairs and a coarse pair.

5 The half-stitch section of the scallops is worked next, using seven pairs and a coarse pair and making pearls along the outside edge, as indicated by the arrows. Weave the coarse thread through from outside to inside at the intersection of the scallops.

Filling
Six Pin Chain and Leadwork (p.104)

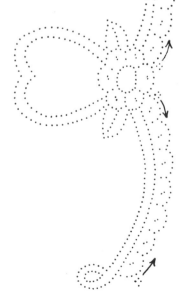

Diagram 8

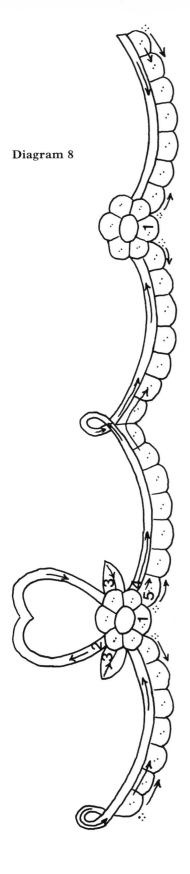

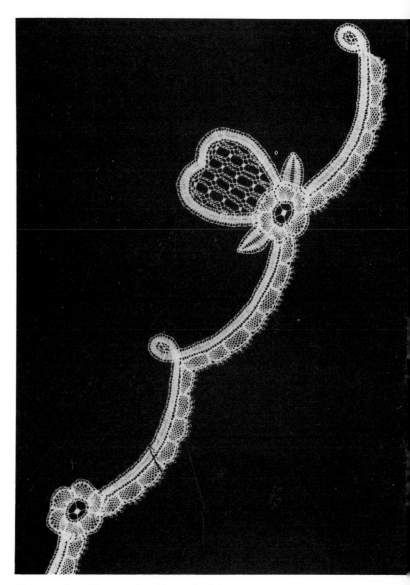

Pattern 8 *Heart and scallop veil edging*

9 *Springtime* (120)

Pricking 9

Diagram 9

The flowers

Work the two large flowers (1) first. Start on the inner whole-stitch section with five pairs and a coarse pair and increase to eight pairs plus the coarse pair at the widest point. Decrease again to five pairs and work out into the half-stitch outer circle of the flower. Increase to nine pairs and a coarse pair and weave the coarse thread through from outside to inside at each intersection of the petals.

Start from the bottom of the stems of each of the flowers (2) and work in rib with six pairs. Work into the half stitch, using seven pairs and a coarse pair. Sew out.

Work all the other flowers in the same way with the same number of pairs.

The leaves

Work the small leaves next, starting with six pairs and a coarse pair and increasing to eight pairs and a coarse pair. Twist the runners once in the centre of the downright to make the vein.

Work the large leaves next. Start the whole-stitch section with six pairs and a coarse pair and increase to 11 pairs and a coarse pair at the widest point, where a four pin bud is worked. Turn the corner with six pairs and a coarse pair. Change to half stitch and increase to nine pairs and the coarse pair at the widest point.

The stems

Work the stems in whole stitch, using six pairs and a coarse pair. Sew out into the leaves.

Fillings

The filling in the large flowers is Blossom (p.92) and Swing Leadworks were used in the small flowers.

Pattern 9   *Springtime (made by Ann Solman)*

27

10 *Floral veil edging* (180)

1 Start the larger section of the two with the large flower. Work the whole-stitch section first, starting with seven pairs and a coarse pair and increasing to ten pairs and a coarse pair. Take out one pair at the end of the last whole-stitch petal and work the rest of the flower in half stitch, making pearls on the outside edge where necessary.

2 Start at the scroll with seven pairs and a coarse pair and increase to 12 pairs at the widest point. Decrease to ten pairs and the coarse pair at the end of the scroll and work into the flower, making pearls where necessary.

3 Work this section with the same number of pairs, again working pearls where necessary, and sew out into the scroll. Work the half-stitch scalloped section between these two pieces next.

Sew 12 pairs into the edge of the lace and hang in a coarse pair. Work in half stitch, weaving the coarse thread through at the intersection of each scallop. Make pearls all the way along the bottom edge.

4 Work the section from the scroll to the flower next in the same way as the previous similar piece, making pearls where necessary. Work the half-stitch bobbles above the flower next, using seven pairs and a coarse pair. Weave the coarse thread across after each section. Cut out the coarse thread at the bottom of the last bobble and change to rib, keeping the pinholes on the outside of the curve. Sew out into the flower.

The small leaves are now worked, starting with seven pairs and a coarse pair and increasing to ten pairs and a coarse pair at the widest point. Make a vein down the centre by twisting the runners three times in the centre of the downrights on each row.

Remove this section from the pillow and begin the next.

5 Work this flower in the same way as the one in the first section. Work the small leaves above the flower in the same way as the previous ones, also the half-stitch bobbles.

For the small flowers, sew in seven pairs at the

Pricking 10

28

base of the stem and work in rib with the pinholes on the outside of the curve. Work up into the flower and weave in a coarse pair before changing to half stitch for the flower. Weave the coarse thread through at the intersection of the petals. Sew out.

6 In order to make this section the previous piece must be pinned on to the pillow where indicated by the dotted lines. Sew in seven pairs and hang in a coarse pair. Work in whole stitch and increase to 11 pairs. Make pearls where necessary. Sew out into the flower.

7 Work the half-stitch scalloped section next as on the first piece. Make pearls all along the bottom edge. Work the fillings next.

Fillings

No-Pin (p.101) was used to fill the large flowers and Straight Pin (p.105) for the other two sections.

These two pieces when joined together as described make a complete pattern.

Pattern 10 *Floral veil edging*

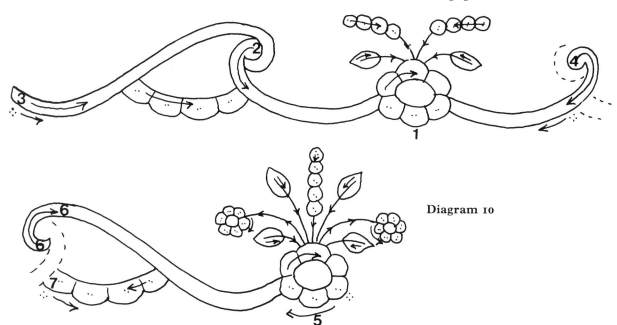

Diagram 10

29

11 *Easter chick* (120)

Pricking 11

Diagram 11

1 Start this section of the wing with six pairs and a coarse pair. Work in half stitch, increasing to 11 pairs and the coarse pair at the widest point. Decrease to turn the corner at the top of the wing and work along the top towards the tip. It will be necessary to lay back the ends at the tip of the wing to finish off.

2 Work this section in half stitch, starting with six pairs and a coarse pair and increasing to ten pairs at the widest point. Sew out into the first section of the wing.

3 Work in half stitch, starting with eight pairs and a coarse pair and increasing to 16 pairs and the coarse pair at the widest point. Use six pairs for the narrow side of the division and the other ten pairs for the longer, wider section.

4 Start at the centre section of the crest with six pairs and a coarse pair. Work in half stitch and increase to eight pairs and the coarse pair. Change to whole stitch at the top of the head and continue down the head and body. Increase until there are 16 pairs and the coarse pair when working the snatch pin. Continue down the breast and sew out into the wing.

5 and 6 Work these two sections next in half stitch. Start with six pairs and a coarse pair, increase to eight pairs and a coarse pair at the widest point. Sew out into the head, having decreased to five pairs and the coarse pair.

7 and 8 Work the beak in whole stitch, starting with five pairs and a coarse pair and adding one pair as it widens. Sew out into the head.

9 Start at the top of the tail section with six pairs and a coarse pair. Work in half stitch with pearls on the outside of the curve. Increase to eight pairs and the coarse pair and then decrease to six pairs and the coarse pair for the narrow part of the tail.

10 Work this part of the tail next in the same way as the first.

11 and 12 Work the feet in whole stitch,

Pattern 11 *Easter chick*

starting with five pairs and a coarse pair and increasing to six and the coarse pair. Sew out into the body.

13 This part of the branch is worked in whole stitch. Start with six pairs and a coarse pair and increase to ten pairs and the coarse pair at the widest point. Sew into the feet, working over them and finishing by sewing into the bottom of the wing.

14 This section is worked now in the same way as the first piece of the branch. The remaining branches are also worked in a similar fashion.

12 *Wild strawberries* (120)

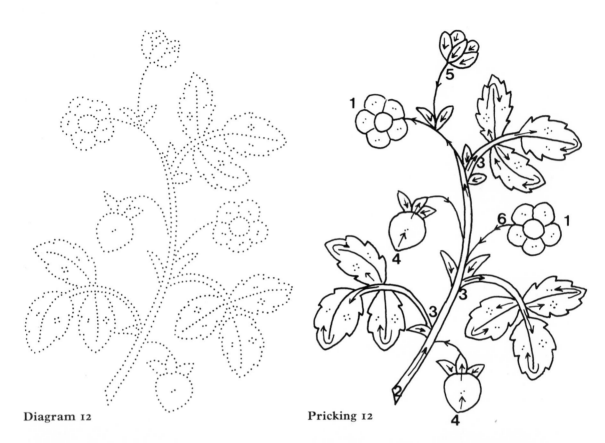

Diagram 12

Pricking 12

1 Work the two flowers in half stitch using eight pairs and a coarse pair.

2 Work the main stem in whole stitch, starting with six pairs and a coarse pair. Add one more pair as it widens and take it out again as the stem narrows, and also one more pair further up the stem. Remove the coarse pair, change to rib, keeping the pinholes on the outside of the curve. Sew out into the flower.

3 To work the leaves, sew five pairs into the main stem, hang in a coarse pair and work in whole stitch up the leaf stem and into the whole-stitch side of the leaf. Add and take out one extra pair on the outside edge before and after the points are worked as necessary. Increase to ten pairs and a coarse pair at the widest part and decrease to six pairs and a coarse pair to work around the tip of the leaf. Change to half stitch, sewing into the whole-stitch section and increasing to eight pairs and a coarse pair at the widest part. For the side leaves, sew into the stem and work up the whole-stitch section and down the half-stitch one. Sew into the stem, cross over it and again work up the whole-stitch section and down the half-stitch section.

All the leaves are worked in a similar way, using the same numbers of bobbins or a few less for any narrower leaves.

4 To work the strawberries start at the tip with six pairs and a coarse pair. Work in half stitch, increasing to 11 pairs and a coarse pair at the widest part. Decrease to six pairs and the coarse

Pattern 12 *Wild strawberries*

pair for the calyx. Cut out the coarse pair at the end tip and continue in rib for the stem.

The remaining two calyxes and the ones at the base of the leaf stems are worked in whole stitch, using six pairs and a coarse pair.

5 For the bud, start at the tip of the central calyx with six pairs and a coarse pair and work in whole stitch.

At the bottom cut out the coarse pair and continue in rib to the flower stem. Sew out the pairs.

Work the other two calyxes with six pairs and the coarse pair; sew out into the central calyx.

For the two half-stitch petals, use six pairs and a coarse pair.

6 Work this flower stem with six pairs, sewing into the flower and working in rib with the pinholes on the left, and sew out into the main stem.

Filling
Blossom (p.92)

13 *Vintage car* (120)

1 Commence the wheel with a straight start. Work in whole stitch, using nine pairs and a coarse pair.

2 Work the second wheel in the same way.

3 Work the back bumper in whole stitch with a maximum of seven pairs and a coarse pair.

4 Start the mudguard with six pairs and a coarse pair. Work in whole stitch and increase to seven pairs and a coarse pair. Sew out into the bumper.

5 Work the hood in whole stitch with six pairs and a coarse pair. Add one more pair where it widens.

6 Work the bar down the centre of the hood with five pairs and a coarse pair.

7 Work Italian Filling (p.99) in the hood.

8 Use six pairs and a coarse pair for the axle and work it in whole stitch.

9 Work the outline of the bonnet in whole stitch, with a maximum of nine pairs and a coarse pair.

10 Work this section in whole stitch with six pairs and a coarse pair.

Pricking 13

Diagram 13

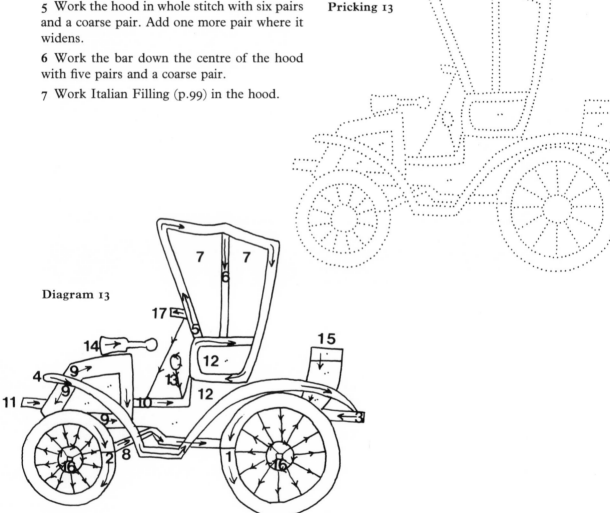

34

Pattern 13   *Vintage car (designed by Mr Stedman and made by Tina Jackson)*

11 Work the front bumper in whole stitch with six pairs and a coarse pair.

12 Fill in the half-stitch section of the car by sewing pairs into the outline of the body.

13 Work the hand brake in rib with five pairs.

14 Work the lamp with a straight start at the front and work in whole stitch carefully laying back the ends at the end.

15 Make the seat at the back with a straight start and use 12 pairs and a coarse pair. Weave the coarse thread through at the end of the whole-stitch section and work in half stitch, sewing out into the bumper. Work the section under the bumper by sewing in pairs and hanging in a coarse pair. Sew out into the wheel.

16 Work the hub in the centre of the wheels with five pairs in rib. Join to the start and work down the adjacent spoke. The spokes are all worked with five pairs in rib and sewn out into the wheel. Make swing leadworks to fill the centre of the hubs.

17 Work the steering wheel in whole stitch with six pairs and a coarse pair. Rib down the column with six pairs.

14 Mrs Rabbit (180)

1 Start at the front edge of the hat brim in whole stitch, using six pairs and a coarse pair and increase to eight pairs and the coarse pair at the widest part. Reduce again to six pairs and the coarse pair and lay back the ends at the tip.

2 Work the ear in whole stitch, starting with six pairs and the coarse pair, increasing to ten pairs and the coarse pair, and sew out into the hat brim.

3 Start at the top of the hat with seven pairs and the coarse pair. Work in half stitch, increasing to 11 pairs and the coarse pair. Weave the coarse thread through before and after working the whole-stitch band. Sew out into the brim.

4 Start at the nose with seven pairs plus the coarse pair and increase to 17 pairs and the coarse pair. Work in whole stitch, making a snatch-pin hole for the eye. Sew out.

5 Work the collar in half stitch, starting at the front tip with seven pairs and the coarse pair, increasing to nine pairs and the coarse pair. Sew out into the brim of the hat.

6 Start the sleeve at the shoulder end with seven pairs and a coarse pair. Work in whole stitch and increase to 11 pairs. Weave the coarse thread through before and after the half-stitch cuff. Work the hand in whole stitch. Weave the coarse thread through at the end of the hand and carry on to make the leaf with a central vein, laying back the ends at the top of the leaf.

7 Start the bodice at the top of the arm, as indicated, with six pairs and a coarse pair and increase to 11 pairs and the coarse pair. Work this in half stitch.

8 Work the peplum, starting with the centre section. Sew into the bodice and work in whole stitch, starting with six pairs and the coarse pair, increasing to eight pairs and the coarse pair and decreasing again to six pairs and the coarse pair, and sew out into the bodice.

9 and 10 Work these two sections in whole

Pricking 14

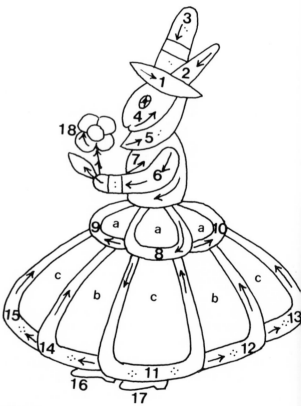

Diagram 14

36

Pattern 14 *Mrs Rabbit*

stitch. Sew seven pairs and the coarse pair into the centre section and reduce to six pairs and the coarse pair. Sew out into the bodice.

11 The skirt sections are worked next. Start with the centre one with seven pairs and the coarse pair and increase to 11 pairs and the coarse pair. Work in whole stitch, making two four pin buds along the bottom edge.

Sew 11 pairs and a coarse pair into the bottom of the centre panel and decrease to seven pairs and the coarse pair at the bodice. Work in whole stitch. Sections 12, 13, 14 and 15 are all worked in the same way.

16 and 17 Work the shoes in whole stitch with eight pairs and the coarse pair.

18 Sew seven pairs into the hand and work the stem of the flower in rib. Work into the flower and add a coarse pair. Make a swing leadwork in the centre of the flower.

Fillings
a   No Pin (p.101)
b   Brick (p.93)
c   Toad in the Hole with Wide Leadworks (p.110)

37

two

PARTLY RAISED PATTERNS

15 *Sailing ship* (120)

1 Start with six pairs and a coarse pair and work the outlines of the ship in whole stitch. Increase to seven pairs and a coarse pair as the section widens.

Weave the coarse thread through at the intersection of each of the scallops along the top of the ship. Sew out.

2 Start at the tip of the scroll with six pairs and work in rib until the wave widens. Weave in a coarse pair and continue in whole stitch until the start of the rib at the end of the wave. Cut out the coarse pair and work in rib, sewing out at the end of the scroll. Work the remaining waves in the same way.

3 Start at the bottom edge of the flag on the main mast. Work in rib with six pairs around the flag and down the mast.

4 Work this section in rib with six pairs.

5 Start this section with six pairs plus one coarse thread and one other with it to make a pair. Work in whole stitch and sew out into the top of the ship. The maximum number of pairs used will be 11, plus one coarse and one other to make the pair.

6 Work this section in the same way as the previous one, but in half stitch. Use a maximum of nine pairs, plus one coarse and one other.

7 **and** 8 Work these sections in rib, with six pairs, in the direction indicated. Sew into the mast before and after ribbing around the crow's-nest.

9 Rib down the stern of the ship, hanging in four pairs to be used with the rib pairs to fill in the ship with half stitch.

10 Start at the bottom edge of the flag with six pairs.

Rib around the flag and down the flag-pole.

Pricking 15

Diagram 15

Pattern 15 *Sailing ship*

16 Arum lily (120)

The lily

Start at 1 with six pairs and a coarse pair and work in whole stitch, increasing to eight pairs at the widest part. Decrease to six pairs again as the pattern narrows, sew out and lay back the pairs at 2.

Using six pairs, rib from 3 to the base and leave the pairs. Rib from 4 to the base and leave the pairs. Sew out and tie off three outer pairs of the 12 on each side.

Sew into the base as many of the remaining pairs as possible, and use these with a coarse pair to make the stem of the lily. Add pairs as this widens into the flower to 11 pairs and the coarse pair. Decrease to nine pairs on the side of the lily and six pairs at the top. Tie the pairs at the top pinhole and continue down the other side of the flower, sewing out at 5.

Work the leaves next.

The leaves

Start at 6 with six pairs and a coarse pair. Work in whole stitch, adding and taking out pairs as required. Make raised sewings into the central rib, being careful to tie at the top pinhole. Change to half stitch and finish by sewing at 7. Repeat these instructions for the other leaf.

The spadix

Start the spadix with six pairs and the coarse pair, increasing to eight pairs plus the coarse pair, decrease as it widens at the bottom and sew out at 11. Sew two pairs in the pair of adjacent top holes (12), and work in half stitch, increasing to 13 pairs at the widest point, top sewing into the sides of the lily. (Work over the top of the spadix.)

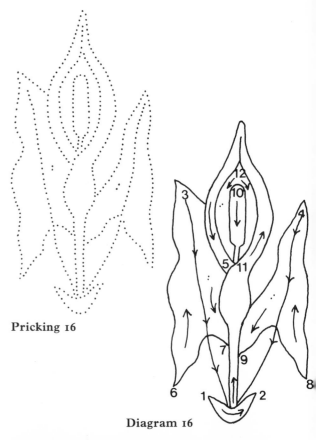

Pricking 16

Diagram 16

Pattern 16   *Arum lily*

17 Hart's tongue fern (120)

Leaf A
Start at 1 with six pairs and a coarse pair. Work up the stem in whole stitch and into the leaf, increasing to nine pairs plus the coarse pair at the widest point. Decrease to six pairs at the tip. Tie at the top pinhole. Work down the other side of the leaf in half stitch, adding one more pair (seven pairs in all), and sew out at 2.

Leaf B
Start at 3 with six pairs and work in rib, then add a coarse pair where the vein widens, by weaving it through the downrights and laying back until the first whole-stitch row is completed, when it is brought into position. Sew out into the stem of leaf A.

Start again at 4 with eight pairs and a coarse pair. Work up the leaf in whole stitch, adding and taking out as required, and top sewing into the vein. Tie at the top pinhole and work down the other side in half stitch, adding and taking out pairs as required, and sew out into the stem at 5.

Leaf C
Repeat as for leaf B, sewing into the vein and adjoining leaves where necessary.

Leaf D
Start at 9 with six pairs and a coarse pair, increasing to 11 pairs and the coarse pair. Twist twice for the central vein and sew out into the stem, having decreased to six pairs and the coarse pair.

Leaf E
Start at 11 and sew out at 12, working in a similar manner to leaf D.

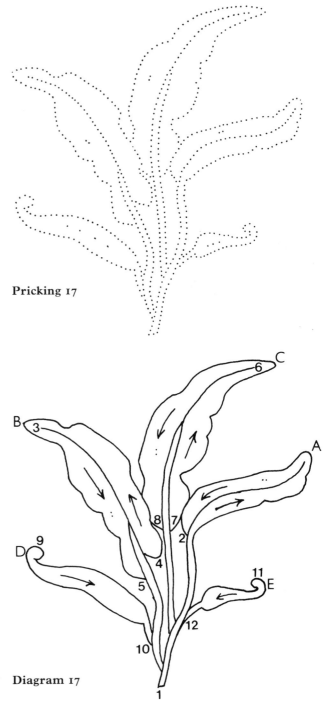

Pricking 17

Diagram 17

Pattern 17   *Hart's tongue fern*

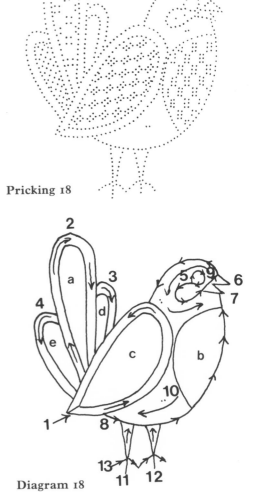

Pricking 18

Diagram 18

18 Robin (180)

1 Start at the tip of the wing with six pairs and the coarse pair. Increase to eight pairs plus the coarse pair and work around the wing in whole stitch.

2 Work the central tail section next. Sew in six pairs and hang in the coarse pair into the wing, working in whole stitch, and sew out into the wing.

3 and 4 The left- and right-hand sections of the tail are now worked. In each case, sew seven pairs into the tail and hang in the coarse pair. Work in whole stitch, decreasing to six pairs and the coarse pair, and sew out into the wing.

5 Starting at the corner of the eye with seven pairs, rib around the eye, cheek and head and sew out into the wing.

6 Work the top section of the beak with six pairs plus the coarse pair. Sew out into the rib, cut out the coarse pair and leave the other pairs for the half-stitch head.

7 Work the bottom section of the beak in whole stitch, starting with five pairs and the coarse pair and adding one pair as it widens. Sew out into the rib.

8 Sew seven pairs into the bottom of the wing and rib up to the bottom section of the beak.

9 Using the six pairs left from the top section of the beak, work the half stitch around the head. Take out one pair over the top of the eye, then add three pairs where it widens and sew out carefully into the rib at the bottom of the beak.

10 Sew in 15 pairs along the bottom edge of the breast and work in half stitch, decreasing as the section narrows.

11 Start the foot with seven pairs and rib to the bottom of the leg, weave in a coarse pair, working in whole stitch, and sew out into the body.

12 Work the second leg in the same way.

13 Start at the tip of the toe with seven pairs and rib to the foot, sew in and continue to rib to the next foot. Sew into the foot and continue the rib to the tip of the last foot, carefully laying back ends and tying off.

Work two swing leadworks in the cheek.

Fillings

a Four Pin Flower and Leadwork (p.97)
b Toad in the Hole with Enclosed Pins (p.109)
c Toad in the Hole with Wide Leadworks (p.110)
d No Pin (p.101)
e Pin and a Stitch (p.102)

Pattern 18 *Robin*

19 Collar (180)

The centre panel has to be worked first.

1 Work in whole stitch with seven pairs and a coarse pair and sew out at the end of the section.

2 Start half stitch in a straight line, adding pearls on the outside edge. Use ten pairs and a coarse pair. Weave the coarse thread through at the end of each scallop. Always weave from the outside to the inside and back, to follow the line of the scallop. Sew out into the whole stitch section.

3 Work the inner rib circle of the flower next, using seven pairs of bobbins. Join up the ring, without taking out the pin, and work out into the whole stitch, adding a coarse pair.

Add pairs until there are 13 and the coarse pair. Work the first three petals in whole stitch and the second three in half stitch. Weave the coarse thread through after each scallop. For the half stitch petals, reduce to 11 pairs and the coarse pair. Swing and Stitch filling was used for the centre of the flower.

4 Start at 4 and rib around the circles, always keeping the pinholes on the outside of the curve. Sew into the start and rib down the stem.

5 Raise the leaves along the bottom edge with a rib of seven pairs. Work back over the leaf, adding one more pair. Work in whole stitch with a vein in the middle. Reduce to seven pairs at the bottom and sew into the stem. Use the same pairs to rib up the second leaf and work back and sew out into the stem. Work the other leaves in the same way.

6 Start the petal, where indicated, with seven pairs and a coarse pair, add two pairs and work around the flower, making windows where shown. Sew out.

7 Start at the top circle with seven pairs and a coarse pair. Work in half stitch and weave the coarse thread through at the end of each circle. One more pair will have to be added for the last two, slightly larger circles.

Cut out one pair and the coarse pair before ribbing to the flower, then sew out.

8 Sew seven pairs and a coarse pair into the

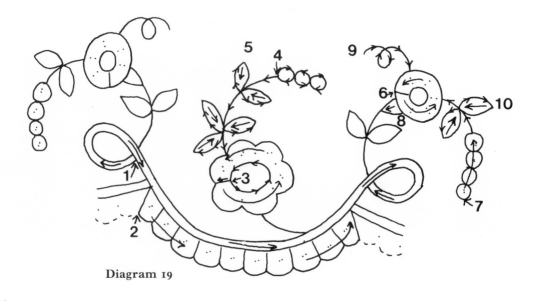

Diagram 19

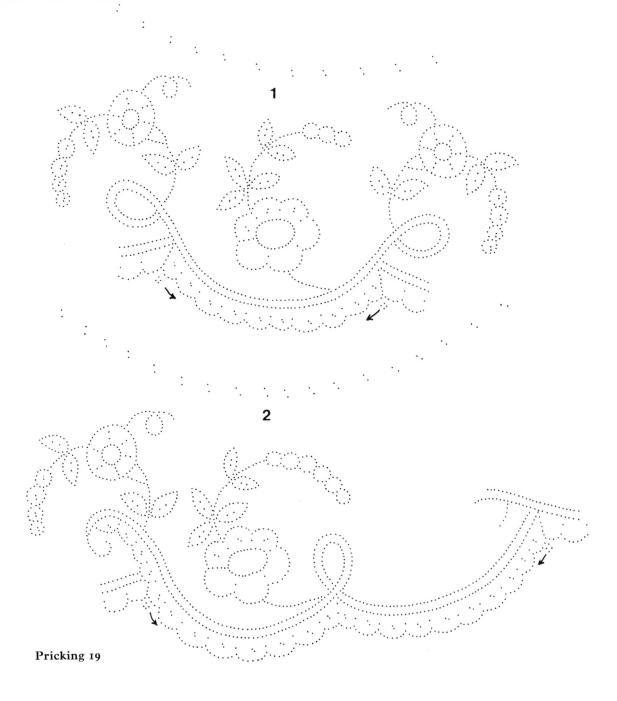

1

2

Pricking 19

flower edge and work in whole stitch to the top of the stem. Cut out the coarse pair and continue in rib to the outside edge of the collar.

9 Start at the top of the tendril with seven pairs and rib to the flower.

10 Make leaves as for 5. The opposite spray is made in the same way.

Make the other sections of the collar in the order indicated. Sew each section into the previous one as you work until they are all completed.

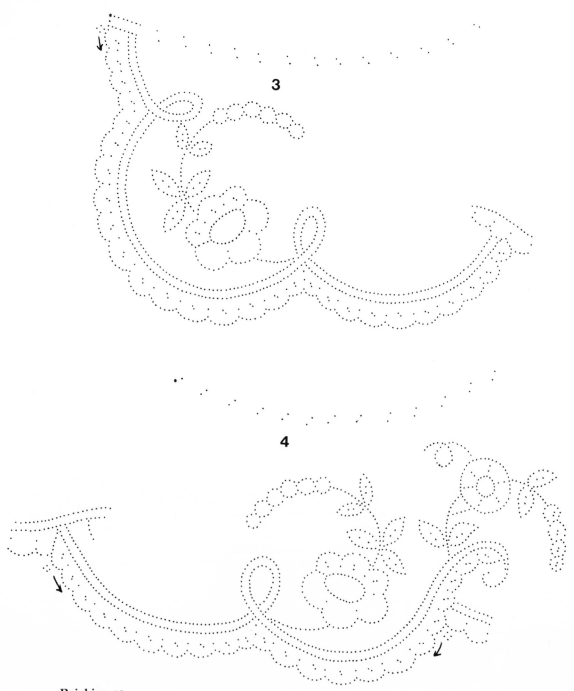

3

4

Pricking 19

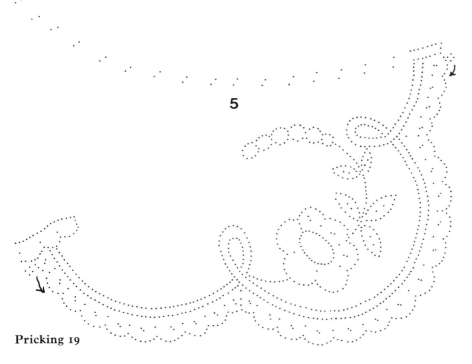

5

Pricking 19

Pattern 19 *Collar*

20 *Apple* (120)

(Before starting this pattern make sure all the knots are wound well on.)

1 Start at the top of the stem with six pairs plus a coarse pair. Work in whole stitch and, as the centre of the core widens, add until there are 11 pairs and the coarse pair.

To work the leadworks in the centre of the core, work through to the middle of the downrights and then through two pairs more.

Leave the runners and take the last pair of bobbins worked back through two pairs and leave them. Make a whole stitch with the pair left in the centre, twist them both three times and put in a pin between the pairs.

With the runners left on either side of these pairs, work out to the edge and make a usual pinhole edge. Work back to the centre, twist the runners once and leave them. Take out to the edge and back again to the centre the last pair worked through as new runners. Do this three times on each side.

Make a leadwork with the two pairs left hanging on the pin in the centre, until it reaches the next centre pin. Twist both pairs three times, put in a pin and enclose it with a whole stitch.

Take one of the runners left at the centre and work through the two pairs from the leadwork and the other runners. Leave this pair of bobbins, which now become downrights.

Take the last pair worked through (the other pair of runners), and work out to the edge, where the usual edge stitch is made, and the whole stitch continues until the next pair of leadworks is reached. These are worked in the same way, but leaving four pairs in the centre for the two leadworks instead of the two pairs as described above.

2 Decrease to seven pairs at the bottom of the central core and work up section 2 in whole stitch, with pearls on the inner edge. Increase to ten pairs and a coarse pair at the widest point.

Decrease to seven pairs at the top and cut out the coarse pair.

3 The last part of this section is worked in rib, which is sewn into the top of the core, and then the same pairs are used to rib down section 3.

4 Sew in at the bottom of the core and use these pairs to rib up section 4.

5 Sew in the pairs at the top of the core, add a coarse pair and use the same pairs to work the half-stitch section 5. Increase to 11 pairs and the coarse pair at the widest point. Decrease to seven pairs at the end of the half stitch, cut out the coarse pair and continue in rib.

6 Sew out into the core and use the same pairs to work in half stitch up section 6. Increase to ten pairs at the widest point. Sew out into the core, tie all the pairs and cut them off.

Work the two leaves next.

Leaves

Sew five pairs into the core and hang in a coarse pair. Work up the whole-stitch section, first increasing to 11 pairs and a coarse pair at the widest point. Work the four pin bud and decrease to five pairs and the coarse pair to work around the point. Tie the pair at the point and continue the half-stitch section, increasing to eight pairs and the coarse pair at the widest point. Sew out into the stem.

Scalloped bottom

To work the scalloped piece at the bottom of the apple, sew in five pairs and hang in a coarse pair. Work in whole stitch, taking the coarse thread across to divide the scallops. Increase to nine pairs and the coarse pair at the widest point. Decrease again to five pairs and the coarse pair and sew out.

The fillings are now worked.

Pricking 20

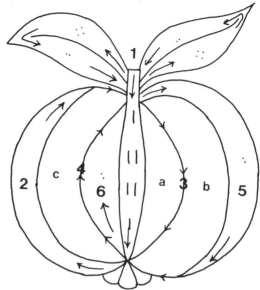

Diagram 20

Fillings

Those used in this pattern were:

a Pin and a Stitch with Leadworks (p.103)
b Whole Stitch Block (p.113)
c Diamond (p.95)

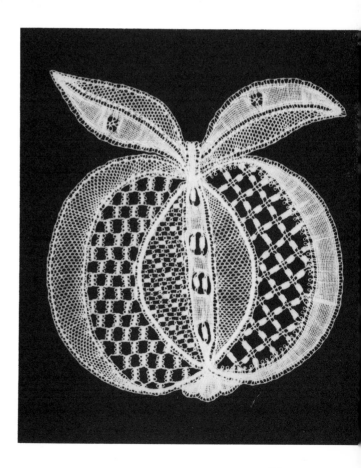

Pattern 20 *Apple*

21 Small tiger lily (120)

1 Start at the top of the right-hand stamen, with five pairs, and work in rib to the centre of the flower. Leave these bobbins.

2 Start the central whole-stitch ring with six pairs and the coarse pair. Work past the bottom of the stamen and leave the pairs. Finish off the stamen and sew out into the ring. Work the other stamens next in the same way. Finish off the ring by working over the top of the stamens.

3 The centre, whole-stitch part of the petals is worked next. Start at the tip with six pairs and work in rib until it widens. Weave in a coarse pair and add one more pair as the section widens. Sew out into the centre ring.

4 Sew five pairs into the central ring and work in half stitch with just one coarse thread on the outside edge. It will be necessary to increase and decrease as the work widens and narrows. Five pairs will be the minimum number of bobbins needed and eight pairs the maximum. (There will be one extra bobbin to make up for only having one coarse thread.) Work the petals in the order shown on the diagram – 4,5,6,7 and 8.

9 Work the stem in whole stitch, starting at the bottom tip and finishing at the petal, using seven and then eight pairs plus the coarse pair.

10 and 11 The leaves are worked next. With seven pairs for each one, make the veins, starting at the tip and finishing at the stem. Sew in 11 pairs and hang one fine thread and one coarse thread into the stem, and work the half-stitch section of the leaf, adding one more pair as it widens and decreasing to five pairs at the tip. Work the whole-stitch section with nine pairs and the coarse pair. (It will be necessary to attach the vein in each section every three holes when working over them.)

Pricking 21

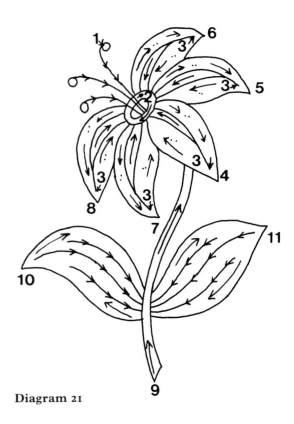

Diagram 21

Pattern 21 *Small tiger lily*

22 Fuschia and butterfly spray

Pattern 22 *Fuschia and butterfly spray*

1 Start by making the two antennae in rib using four pairs, with the pinholes on the left. Use all but one of these pairs and a coarse pair for the body of the butterfly.

2 Work this part of the wing next, using six pairs for the rib.

3 Rib around this part of the wing in the same way.

4 This section of the wing is worked next in half stitch using a maximum of 11 pairs and a coarse pair.

5 The main stem is worked next, using a maximum of seven pairs and a coarse pair. Work in whole stitch.

6 and 7 This leaf is worked by ribbing down the centre and along the stem, changing to whole-stitch braid for the wider part of the stem and adding a coarse pair. Leave the pairs at the end of the stem while leaf 7 is worked. The stem of leaf 6 can now be finished off on to leaf 7.

All the leaves are worked by first ribbing the central vein, then working the whole-stitch section and, lastly, the half-stitch section. The leaves vary slightly in size but a maximum of ten pairs and a coarse pair is used for the whole-stitch side and eight pairs and the coarse for the half-stitch side.

The flowers

The large flower was started with the right-hand whole-stitch section, using a maximum of ten pairs and the coarse pair. Reduce to six pairs for the rib stem (having cut out the coarse pair). The other whole-stitch section of the flower can then be worked and, lastly, the half-stitch underskirt, starting with the centre section. The stamens are worked last using four pairs.

The smaller flower is worked in a similar way.

The buds

The maximum number of pairs used for the buds was 12, ten and eight pairs plus a coarse pair. The coarse thread is woven through after the first two sections and cut out before working the stem in rib.

Fillings

The filling used for the butterfly wings is Four Pin Flower and Leadwork (p.97).

Pricking 22

Diagram 22

55

three
RAISED PATTERNS

23 Perryman sampler (120)

Pattern 23 *Perryman sampler (made by Margaret Wright)*

1 Start at the inner circle of the central flower with six pairs and a coarse pair, working in whole stitch.

2 Work the outer section of the flower in half stitch using 12 pairs plus the coarse pair. (Instruction will now only be given for one side of the pattern as both sides are identical.)

3 This section is now worked in whole stitch, using eight pairs and a coarse pair.

4 Work in whole stitch, using eight pairs plus the coarse pair, decreasing to six pairs and the coarse pair.

5 Work in whole stitch, starting with six pairs and the coarse pair, increasing to eight pairs and the coarse pair as it widens. Reduce to six pairs and the coarse pair again before sewing out.

6 The raised leaf with taps is worked with six pairs for the rib and eight pairs for the leaf sections.

7 This leaf has a central ribbed vein. The whole-stitch side is worked using ten pairs and a coarse pair and the half-stitch side using nine pairs and a coarse pair.

8 Work the whole-stitch section of the leaf using 11 pairs and a coarse pair and the half-stitch section with nine pairs and a coarse pair. Work sections 9, 10, 11, and 12 in whole stitch, using six pairs and a coarse pair.

Fillings
a   Diamond (p.95)
b   Four Pin (p.96)
c   Straight Pin (p.105)
d   Blossom (p.92)
e   Whole Stitch Block Variation (p.114)
f   Toad in the Hole (p.108)
g   Trolly Net (p.112)

Pricking 23

Diagram 23

59

24 *Voysey sampler* (120)

Start at the square end of the heart (1), using seven pairs and a coarse pair. Work in whole stitch. Work the heart and one loop and leave the pairs. Start the next heart in the same way and when the first loop has been made it will be possible to finish off the first bobbins left from the previous section. The whole of the outline is worked in this way.

A　Use six pairs for the rib and a maximum of 12 pairs for the whole-stitch side and nine pairs for the half stitch.

B　For the ten-sectioned leaf use six pairs for the rib and a maximum of eight pairs for each of the whole- and half-stitch sections.

C　Rib around the outside edge using four pairs. Sew in pairs at the top point and work part in whole stitch and part in half stitch with a maximum of seven pairs on each side.

D　Rib around the centre of the leaf with five pairs. Start at the tip of the leaf and work part in whole stitch and part in half stitch. Divide the pairs at the top of the rib and work down each side using a maximum of seven pairs.

　Work the fillings.

Pattern 24　*Voysey sampler (made by Tina Jackson)*

Fillings

a　Six Pin Chain and Leadworks (p.104)
b　Blossom (p.92)
c　Toad in the Hole (p.108)
d　Leadworks and Lattice (p.100)
e　Four Pin Lattice (p.98)
f　Brick Variation (p.94)
g　Pin and a Stitch (p.102)
h　Straight Pin (p.105)
i　Toad in the Hole with Enclosed Pins (p.109)
j　Four Pin (p.96)
k　Toad in the Hole Variation (p.111)
l　Brick (p.93)
m　Trolly Net (p.112)

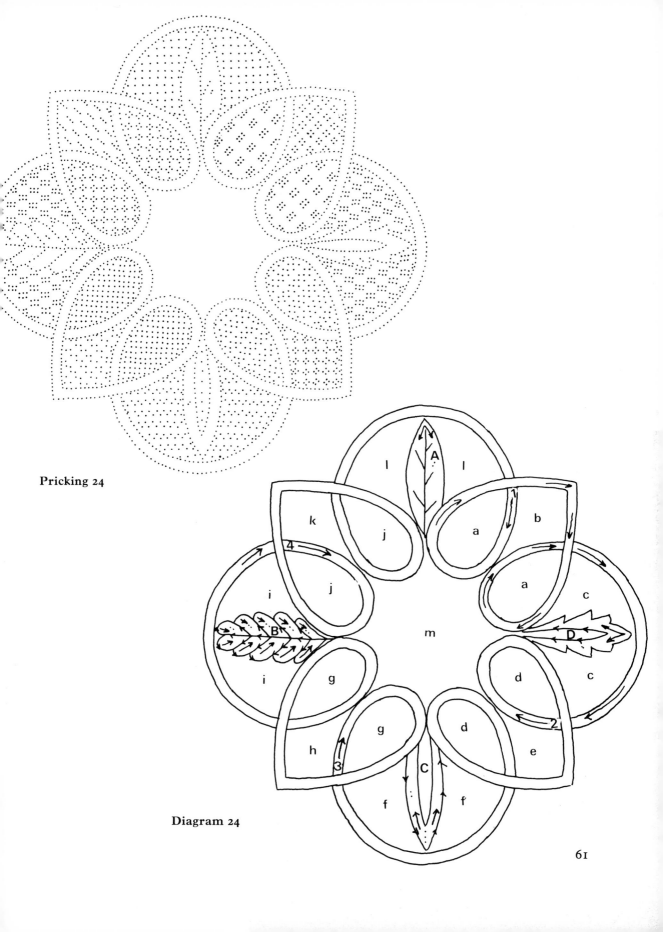

Pricking 24

Diagram 24

25 *Turkey* (120)

1 Start with five pairs and work in rib from the cheek, around the beak and head, down the neck and sew out into the cheek.

2 Sew in five pairs at the tip of the beak and fill in with whole stitch, increasing to eight pairs. Where the beak joins the face, twist the downrights twice and continue in whole stitch up the face to the eye. Have 16 pairs at the beginning of the eye, work the snatch pin hole, and finish at the back of the face with 13 pairs.

3 Start at the point where the neck joins the cheek with five pairs. Work the neck in whole stitch, using a maximum of 15 pairs. Decrease to four pairs at the bottom and leave these to work the breast front.

4 Start with six pairs and a coarse pair and work section 4, increasing to eight pairs and a coarse pair at the widest part. Leave these pairs.

5 Use the pairs left previously and sew out this section on to section 4.

6 Sew in six pairs, hang in a coarse pair and work this section ending at the neck.

7, 8 **and** 9 Work wing loops 7, 8, and 9 next, using a maximum of six pairs and the coarse pair and a minimum of five pairs and the coarse pair.

a–k The small raised feather sections are made next. Sew six pairs into section 6 and rib along the top of section (a), hanging on an extra five pairs along the top to use for the half stitch. Each section is ribbed and rolled using the following number of pairs: (b) 13 pairs; (c) 12 pairs; (d) 14 pairs; (e) eight pairs; (f) eight pairs; (g) ten pairs; (h) eight pairs; (i) nine pairs; (j) eight pairs; (k) nine pairs. These sections are worked in alternate whole stitch and half stitch, as shown in the diagram, with four pin buds in the whole-stitch sections.

10 Sew into the top of the wing and work the tail sections in whole stitch, with seven pairs and a coarse pair. Use five pairs and the coarse pair to turn at the bottom of each section.

Pricking 25

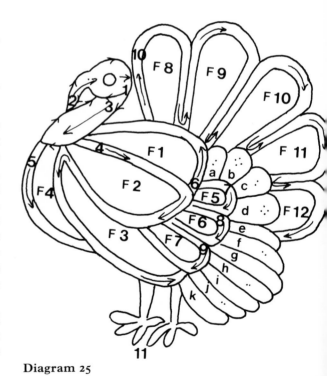

Diagram 25

11 Work the feet next. Start at the centre claw and work up the leg. Work the other claws and finish them on to the first one.

Work the fillings

The fillings

F1 Toad in the Hole with Wide Leadworks (p.110)
F2 Toad in the Hole (p.108)
F3 Diamond (p.95)
F4 Four Pin (p.96)
F5 No Pin (p.101)
F6 Swing and a Stitch (p.107)
F7 Swing and a Pin (p.106)
F8 Leadworks and Lattice (p.100)
F9 Four Pin Lattice (p.98)
F10 Straight Pin (p.105)
F11 Blossom (p.92)
F12 Whole Stitch Block Variation (p.114)

Pattern 25 *Turkey (made by Tina Jackson)*

26 Small cross (120)

The cross is ribbed using six pairs, with the pinhole edge on the outside.

On each inside corner, marked with an arrow, it will be necessary to back stitch three times in order for the rib to lie flat.

Sew out into the start without removing the pin.

Four Pin filling is used and a pair of bobbins is sewn in, twisted and sewn out again in a zig-zag fashion to join the thin parts of the cross.

Pricking 26

Diagram 26

Pattern 26 *Small cross*

27 *Small Madonna and Child* (180)

1 Start at the back of the head and work the halo to within two holes of the start and leave the pairs. This is worked in rib with seven pairs.

2 Start at the bottom edge of the face and work in rib with seven pairs. Rib up the face to the top of the head. Hang in a coarse pair and work in whole stitch, increasing to ten pairs and a coarse pair at the widest point. (It is now possible to finish off the halo.)

Decrease as it narrows to seven pairs. Cut out the coarse pair and change to rib for the Child's head. Sew out into the whole stitch.

3 Sew seven pairs into the bottom of the whole-stitch section and rib to the back of the Child's head. Sew in the pairs and use them to fill in the whole-stitch section. Cut out *one* of the bobbins and hang in a coarse thread for the side where there is no rib. Use a maximum of eight pairs, plus one coarse and one other with it to make a pair. Decrease to seven pairs, having cut out the coarse thread, and continue in rib. Sew out into the whole-stitch section at the back of the Madonna's head. Cut out two pairs and use the remaining five to fill in the half-stitch section. Use a maximum of 14 pairs.

4 Sew seven pairs into the front of the Madonna's face and rib to the Child's head. Sew out and use the same pairs for the half stitch.

Pricking 27

Diagram 27

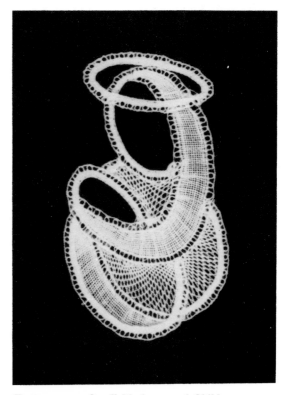

Pattern 27 *Small Madonna and Child (designed by James White)*

28 Kitten (120)

Start at the bottom part of the right eye. Rib around it, using four pairs, keeping the pinhole edge on the left. Sew into the start, without removing the pin, and carry on in rib down one side of the nose, around the face and head, around the second eye and out along the left-hand leg. Use five pairs for all but the eyes, where four pairs only are used.

Sew five pairs into the top of the head, and rib along the top of the body and down around the outside of the tail. Turn at the top and use a maximum of seven pairs to fill in the tail with whole stitch.

Rib along the bottom of the right-hand leg.

Sew 13 pairs along the ribbed bottom edge of the two legs and work in half stitch, filling in the body from here to the tail.

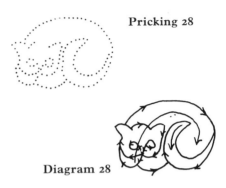

Pricking 28

Diagram 28

Pattern 28 *Kitten*

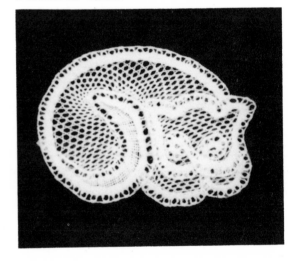

29 *Small spring flower* (180)

Start at the bottom of the stem with seven pairs and rib up the stem with the pinholes on the left. Work down the inside edge of the bottom petal in rib. Turn at the tip and work back in whole stitch, using a maximum of nine pairs. Sew into the rib at the stem having decreased to seven pairs.

Make a roll up the inside edge and rib up to the tip of the second petal. Turn and work back in whole stitch, adding two more pairs for the widest part. Sew out into the first petal.

Sew in seven pairs and hang in a coarse pair to work the half-stitch section of the flower.

Weave the coarse thread through from outside to inside after the first two sections.

Sew seven pairs into the stem and rib up the bottom edge of the right-hand leaf. Turn at the top and work back in whole stitch, twisting the runners three times in the middle to make a vein. Use a maximum of ten pairs at the widest point. Decrease to seven pairs at the bottom, sew out into the stem and use the same pairs to rib the top of the second leaf, and work back in whole stitch in the same way as the first leaf.

Filling

No Pin filling (p.101) was used for the centre of the flower.

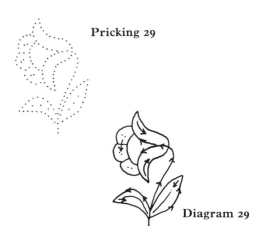

Pricking 29

Diagram 29

Pattern 29 *Small spring flower*

30 Small daisy (120) 31 Madonna and Child (120)

First rib around the central part of the flower using five pairs. Start at the top of the left-hand petal. Rib around and sew into the start, without removing the pin. Carry on in rib with the same pairs down the left-hand edge of the left-hand petal.

Rib along the bottom, hanging in three pairs to be used with the rib pairs for the half stitch. At the bottom, decrease to five pairs and roll down the edge of the first petal. Rib along the bottom edge of the petal, again laying in three pairs, and work in the same way as the first petal.

When working the last half-stitch part of the last petal, sew into the central ring and use the same pairs to fill in the top of the flower with half stitch.

Work the stem in whole stitch with six pairs and a coarse pair.

Rib the bottom edge of each of the leaves, turn at the top and work back in whole stitch, with two twists in the centre of the downrights to make a vein.

Sew out into the stem.

Pricking 30

Diagram 30

Pattern 30
Small daisy

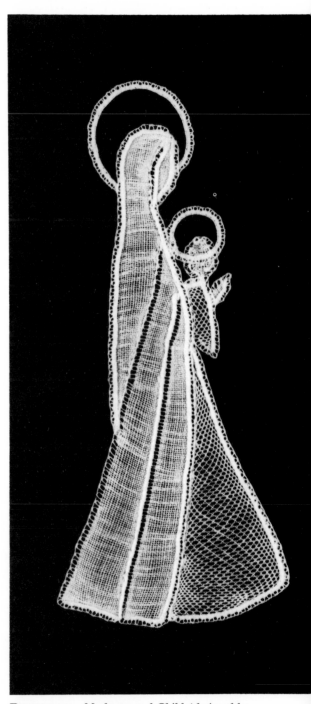

Pattern 31 *Madonna and Child (designed by James White and adapted by V. Pope)*

1 Rib up the face using seven pairs, with the pinholes on the outside edge. Turn at the top and rib down the other side of the face and down the front edge of the cloak. Rib along the bottom, hanging in seven pairs and laying them back to fill in with whole stitch.

2 Work up this section in whole stitch, using 14 pairs in all (seven rib pairs, plus seven layed in).

3 Decrease to seven pairs at the top and use these to roll down the edge. Rib along the bottom, hanging in 11 pairs for the whole stitch (18 pairs in all, including the rib pairs).

4 Work this section in whole stitch and sew out at the top into the rib, but leave the ends long to make sewing into the same place easier later.

5 Sew in seven pairs where indicated and rib up the back of the body. Hang in pairs along the top of the head and lay them back to use later. Sew the rib into the face and use the pairs to fill in the face in whole stitch (6).

7 Fill in the head and body using the pairs hung in when working the rib (12 pairs at the widest point).

8 Rib the Madonna's halo using seven pairs.

9 Hang in seven pairs at the front edge of the cloak and rib down the outside edge of the skirt and along the bottom. Hang in 22 pairs for the half stitch to fill in the skirt while working the rib along the bottom edge.

10 Sew in seven pairs on the cloak at the top of the sleeve. Rib along the top edge, down the front and then turn and fill in the sleeve with whole stitch.

11 Rib along the bottom edge of the hand to the finger tips using seven pairs. Turn at the top and work back in whole stitch.

12 Sew in pairs on the front edge of the cloak and rib the Child's halo. Sew out into the starting point.

13 Start at the top of the Child's head and work in whole stitch. Sew out into the sleeve. Care must be taken when working the head. Do not pull the downrights or the coarse thread too hard or the lace will not remain round in shape.

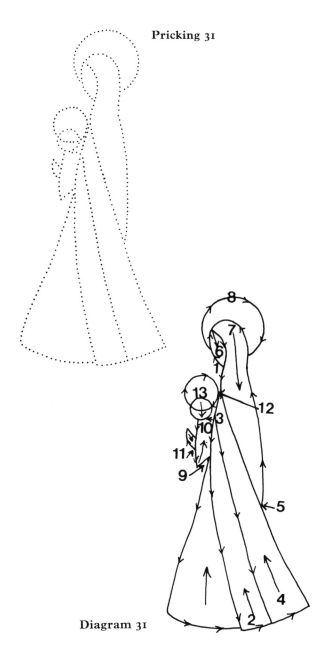

Pricking 31

Diagram 31

32 *Slipper orchid* (180)

1 Start at the tip of the lower leaf with seven pairs and work in rib to where the rib joins the stem. Turn and work back in whole stitch, adding and decreasing as necessary. Turn again at the tip of the leaf and work back along the top in whole stitch, making veins where indicated. Sew out into the leaf.

2 Start at the tip of the stem with seven pairs and a coarse pair. Work in whole stitch and increase to nine pairs and a coarse pair. Sew out into the leaf.

3 Work this leaf in the same way as the first.

4 Sew seven pairs into the bottom leaf, rib up to the bottom of the second leaf. Sew in and work back in whole stitch, sewing out into the first leaf.

5 The flower is worked next. Start on the right with seven pairs and rib up the outside edge. Turn at the top and work down in whole stitch, twisting the runners to make the veins where indicated. Increase to 15 pairs at the widest point. Finish at the bottom with seven pairs and use these to rib the next section (6). Turn at the point and work back in whole stitch, again finishing with seven pairs.

7 Use these pairs to rib around the pouch of the flower, first the outside edge and then the inner one.

8 These same pairs will now be used to rib down the top of this section, work the whole stitch back and sew off.

9 Sew in seven pairs on the left-hand side of section 6 and work in rib to the bottom point, turn and work two rows in whole stitch. Hang five pairs on the other point and work in whole stitch, joining the two sections together. Sew out into section 6.

10 If desired, work the little stamen in the centre of the pouch next, or it could be left out. Work in rib using five pairs. Sew out. Fill in the inner section of the pouch in whole stitch.

11 The half-stitch section is worked using 14 pairs at the widest point.

12 The pairs from the top part of the pouch can now be used to rib down the top of the flower stem. Turn at the bottom and work back in whole stitch. The second flower is worked in the same way.

The second flower is worked in the same way.

13 The two flower sheaths are worked in the same way as the leaves. Start at the tip and work down in rib, turn at the end, work back in whole stitch, turn and work down the inside section making veins where indicated.

14 The flower stems are worked last of all.

Pattern 32 *Slipper orchid*

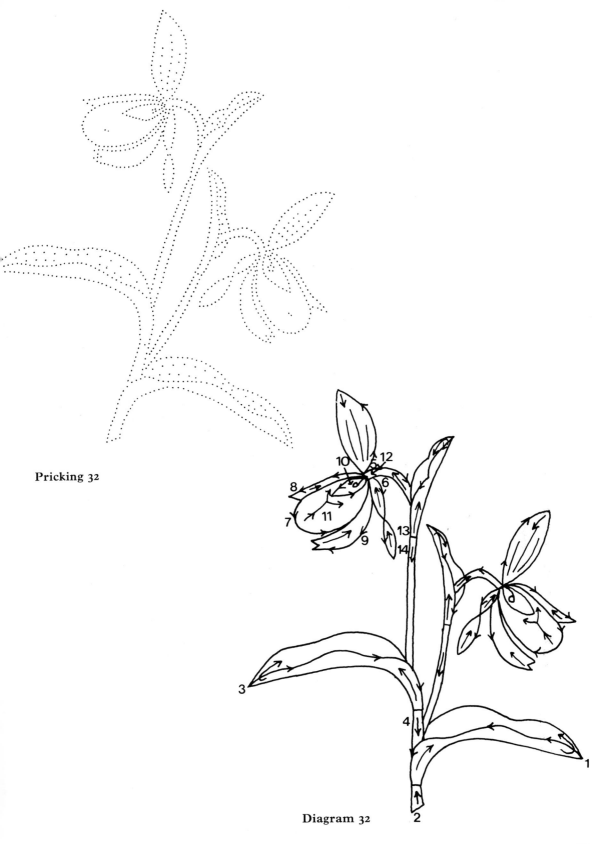

Pricking 32

Diagram 32

33 *Leaf sampler* (120)

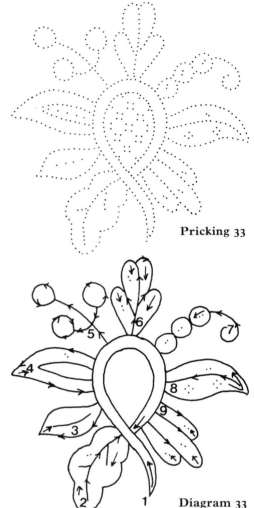

Pricking 33

Diagram 33

1 Start at the point with six pairs and a coarse pair and work in whole stitch. Add one more pair where it widens.

2 Work the ribbed vein first with six pairs. Sew out into the central braid. Sew into this braid and work the whole-stitch section of the leaf, using a maximum of ten pairs, plus a coarse thread and one other with it to make a pair. Turn at the top, sewing into the first hole of the vein without removing the pin. Work down the other side in half stitch, using a maximum of seven pairs, plus a coarse thread, plus one other.

3 Rib up the bottom edge of this leaf with six pairs. Turn at the top and work back in whole stitch with two twists in the centre of the downrights to make a vein. Use a maximum of 13 pairs.

4 Rib around the outside of the leaf with six pairs and sew out into the central braid. Sew in six pairs at the tip and work half in whole stitch and half in half stitch. At the top of the division there must be 14 pairs. These are now divided, using seven pairs for each side. On reaching every other hole at the centre, the runners are both twisted three times. Make a whole stitch with them and put a pin between. Enclose the pin with a whole stitch and three twists, and continue as before.

5 This section is worked in rib with six pairs.

6 Work the central rib of this leaf with six pairs. Turn at the top and work one side of the taps with half stitch, using a maximum of eight pairs. Sew in six pairs at the top of the other side, rib along the top of the first tap and then work down in whole stitch, using a maximum of eight pairs.

7 Start at the tip and work the rib with six pairs. At the first bobble, weave in a coarse pair and change to half stitch. A maximum of eight pairs and the coarse thread will be needed. Weave the coarse thread through at the end of the first two bobbles.

8 Work the central vein with six pairs and sew out into the braid. Use these same pairs to work the whole-stitch side of the leaf, with a maximum of ten pairs, plus one coarse thread and one other with it to make a pair. Work the two four pin buds where indicated. Turn at the top and change to half stitch, using a maximum of six pairs, plus one coarse and one with it to make a pair.

9 This leaf is worked entirely in half stitch, using six pairs for the rib and eight pairs for the taps.

Fillings
Four Pin Flower and Leadwork (p.97)

Pattern 33 *Leaf sampler*

34 *Mouse and wheat* (120)

Wheat

Start at the tip of the bottom ear of wheat 1 with five pairs of bobbins, and work in rib as far as 2.

Add a coarse pair and change to half stitch, adding pairs when necessary, increasing to eight pairs and a coarse pair at the widest part. Take out pairs as it narrows, reducing to six pairs and the coarse pair, cut out this coarse pair, and continue with these six pairs in rib down the stalk. Lay back carefully at the end.

The other ears are worked in a similar manner, each one sewing out into the previous one.

Mouse

Start at A with five pairs of bobbins and rib around the haunch and the back foot. Stop the rib at the third hole down the tail and leave the pairs of bobbins hanging at C.

Start at B on the left ear, with five pairs, and rib around the complete outline of the body, leaving the pairs of bobbins opposite the pairs left at C

Use both sets of five pairs for the first row. Take out two pairs of downrights before commencing the next row. Reduce to six pairs for the thin part of the tail and change to rib. To enable the tail to twine around the stalk, the stalk must now be unpinned temporarily.

Continue with the tail to E and re-pin the stalk, working over it at F. Sew into the stalk and change the pinhole sides on the ribbed tail, which now curves the other way.

Work to G and again unpin the stalk and continue in rib until H. Re-pin the stalk, continue the tail and sew into the stalk. Start at the tip of whisker 3, with five pairs, and work in rib with the holes on the right. Rib to nose and sew into the edge. Change to half stitch and add pairs as necessary.

On reaching the hole for the eye, put three pins into the hole which actually makes a hole in the half stitch. Do not remove these pins until the mouse is completed.

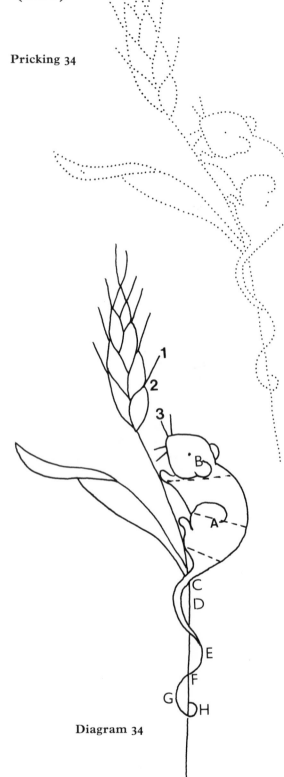

Diagram 34

74

Continue in half stitch, keeping the work at the angle indicated by the dotted lines on the diagram. Do not on any account remove pins A or B. Just lift the pins temporarily while doing the half stitch, making sure the half stitch is evenly spaced on either side of these pins.

Leave the pairs at the first dotted line at the base of the ear, with the runner pair on the right hand side. Sew in six pairs at the top of the paw, and work in half stitch to the level of the other pairs from the body, finishing on the right-hand side. Sew into the rib.

Before commencing the next row from the right with all the pairs, the runner pairs and the pair to the right and left must be crossed, right over left. Continue in half stitch and repeat this process at the hind paw. Sew out the pairs at the base of the tail.

Complete the whiskers, using five pairs of bobbins for each.

Rib the second ear using six pairs of bobbins.

To attach A and B to the half stitch, raise the pin and re-angle it. Use one pair of bobbins and sew into the pinhole, without removing the pin, and through the half stitch. Tie twice and cut off. The reason for doing this at the end instead of while working is that, because of the quantity of bobbins in use, it is difficult to choose the correct place to sew into the pinholes A and B. The leaf may be raised, if wished, but it was not in this case in order to make the mouse the most prominent feature.

Pattern 34 *Mouse and wheat (designed by Lee Ault and made by Tina Jackson)*

35 Siamese cat (120)

Pricking 35

1 Rib around the eye and nose with the plain side of the rib on the outside of the eye. Use six pairs.

2 Start at the tip of the left ear with six pairs and a coarse pair. Work in whole stitch, sewing into the eye and adding one pair. Work around the chin, decreasing to six pairs and the coarse pair. Weave the coarse thread through to indicate the chin, work up the other side of the face and sew out into the eye.

3 Rib along the top of the head with six pairs, laying in pairs for the half stitch centre section of the face. Sew out into the chin (12 pairs, plus the coarse pair, at the widest point).

4 Work the other ear in whole stitch, starting with six pairs and a coarse pair and adding one more pair as it widens. Sew out into the half stitch section of the face.

5 Rib from the top of the haunch, with six pairs, up the left-hand side of the spine and on up to the ear. Sew out the pairs.

6 Sew in seven pairs, plus one coarse bobbin and one other with it to make a pair, into the top of the spine. (The coarse thread will be on the left-hand side.) Work down this section of the back, adding pairs as it widens, with ten pairs at the widest point. Decrease to six pairs at the base of the spine. Sew in and use the same pairs to work up the spine in whole stitch. Increase to eight pairs at the widest point. Sew out at the top of the spine.

7 Work the tail in whole stitch, using eight pairs and a coarse pair. Save the pairs taken out where the tail narrows at the bottom, and use these in the half stitch right-hand section of the body. Sew out into the rib.

8 Use the pairs left at the end of the tail and work the half-stitch section of the body. Increase to 18 pairs near the top of the haunch. At the top of the haunch add a coarse bobbin and one other to make a pair. Work up to the top of the face and sew out.

Diagram 35

9 Work the paw, starting with eight pairs plus a coarse pair and adding one more pair as the leg widens. Sew out into the body.

If you wish to add whiskers, thread a sewing needle with 8 lengths of 120 thread, sew them through the base of the nose and trim to size.

Pattern 35 *Siamese cat*

36 Lapwing (120)

1 With six pairs, rib down the crest, around the face and sew out into the crest. (Leave the ends of the threads long, as the half stitch will sew out into the same place.)

2 Work this section in whole stitch, starting with six pairs and a coarse pair. Increase to 12 pairs and the coarse pair at the widest point. Sew out into the crest.

3 Work the beak in whole stitch, starting with six pairs and a coarse pair, increasing to seven pairs and the coarse pair, and sew out into the face.

4 Sew in eight pairs along the bottom of the face and work in half stitch. Increase to 13 pairs under the eye and to 15 over the eye. Decrease as it narrows and sew out into the crest.

5 Start where indicated with six pairs and rib around the bottom of the wing, around the top and down to the start. Sew in the pairs and use them to work the whole-stitch section of the lower wing, increasing to nine pairs at the widest point. Decrease to five pairs and sew these into the rib, but leave them to complete the first of the rows of scallops across the wing later.

6 Sew in four pairs, hang one coarse and one other bobbin with it to make a pair. Work in whole stitch, dividing the pairs at the face and sewing out into the rib.

7 Use the five pairs left earlier and work the first ribbed scallop across the wing. Sew out into the rib at the top of the wing. Work the remaining scallops in the same way. It will be necessary to back stitch at each point of the scallops in order for the rib to lie flat.

8 Next, fill in the half stitch section of the wing. Sew five pairs into the back of the top of the wing where indicated. Work in half stitch, increasing to 22 pairs at the widest point. Decrease as the section narrows and sew out into the rib at the top of the wing.

9 Start at the tip of the wing with five pairs, sewing them into the rib. Work in whole stitch, twisting for the veins where indicated by the dotted lines on the pattern. Increase to 13 pairs at the widest point. Sew out into the lower wing.

10 Work the tail in whole stitch with a straight start. Use ten pairs, plus one coarse thread and one other to make a pair. (The coarse thread is for the unribbed side.) Make veins where indicated and decrease as the section narrows. Change to half stitch for the under part of the body and increase to 13 pairs and the coarse at the widest part. Sew out into the throat.

11 and 12 For the feet, start with the central toe. Rib, using five pairs. Add a coarse pair and work in whole stitch, increase to seven pairs and the coarse pair at the top of the leg. Sew out into the body. Work the other toes in rib, with five

Pattern 36 *Lapwing*

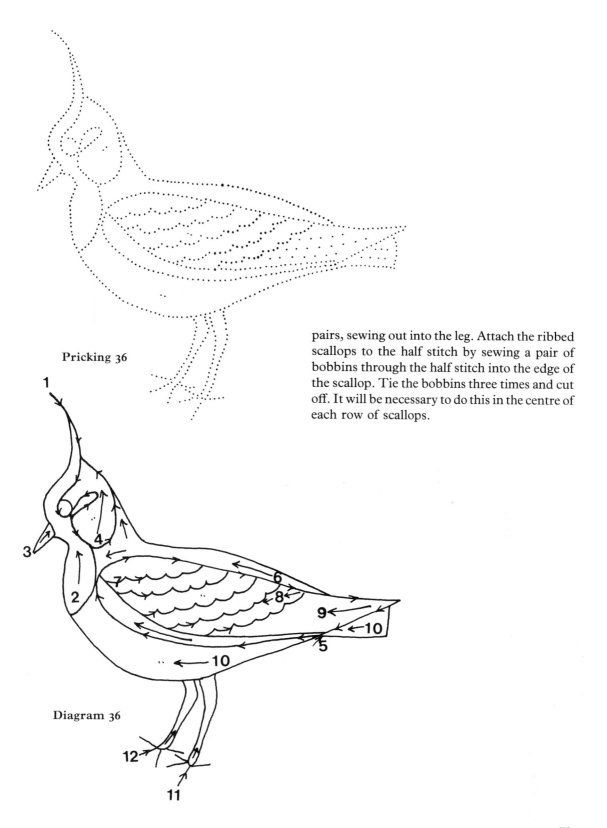

Pricking 36

pairs, sewing out into the leg. Attach the ribbed scallops to the half stitch by sewing a pair of bobbins through the half stitch into the edge of the scallop. Tie the bobbins three times and cut off. It will be necessary to do this in the centre of each row of scallops.

Diagram 36

37 Otter (120)

1 Start at the corner of the right ear with five pairs and rib around the ear and down the face. Continue around the nose, changing the pinhole side of the rib. Sew into the rib at the bottom of the nose and work up around the left-hand eye, towards the right eye. Rib around the eye and sew out into the mouth.

2 Work the fish, starting at the mouth with six pairs and a coarse pair. Work in whole stitch, making a twist in the runners for the mouth and a hole for the eye. Weave the coarse thread through at the end of the head and change to half stitch for the body, using a maximum of eight pairs and the coarse pair. Increase to ten pairs and the coarse pair at the tail and add an extra coarse pair after dividing for the tail. Change to whole stitch and lay the ends back carefully at the end of the two tail sections.

3 Start at the back of the front leg, with six pairs, rib around the leg and sew out into the fish.

4 Sew in six pairs at the side of the left eye, rib around the rest of the body and sew out into the rib of the front leg. Rib the left hand ear.

5 Fill in the body with half stitch. Sew in nine pairs along the front edge of the face and add as the body widens. The dotted lines on the diagram indicate the angle at which the half stitch was worked. The numbers at the end of these same lines show the number of pairs used.

Pattern 37 *Otter*

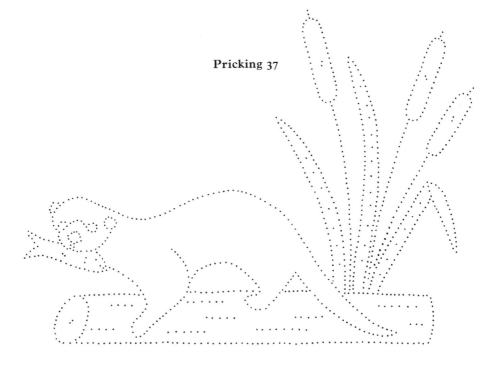

6 Start at the front end of the log and rib as indicated to the other end, sewing to the otter's foot and tail when passing. Hang in 11 pairs when working up the back edge and use all 17 pairs, a coarse thread and one other (to make a pair), and fill in the log with whole stitch. Make twists where indicated, and sew into (a), (b), (c), (d), (e) and (f), when working back over. Change to half stitch for the cut end of the log.

7 Work the three leaves in whole stitch with veins using six pairs and a coarse pair.

8 Start at the tip of the bulrushes with six pairs and rib. Hang in a coarse pair where the bulrush widens, change to half stitch and increase to eight pairs and the coarse pair. Decrease again to six pairs and cut out the coarse pair before working down the stem in rib. Sew out into the log.

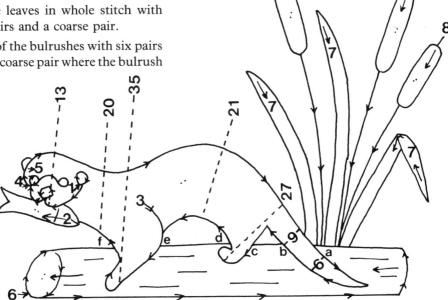

Diagram 37

38 *Prince* (180)

1 Start at the tip of the thumb with seven pairs and work in rib, with the pinholes on the right. Work along the top of the sleeve, down the back of the cloak and leave the pairs at the bottom tip.

2 Sew in seven pairs at the shoulder and rib down the front edge of the cloak with the pinholes on the left. Rib along the bottom of the cloak and sew out into the first rib at the back of the cloak. Use the first lot of pairs and work back the half-stitch under-section of the cloak.

3 Sew seven pairs into the back of the cloak for the scalloped section. It will be necessary to back stitch at the tip of each scallop in order to get it to lie flat. The pinhole edge is on the outside edge of the scallops.

4 Sew into the rib at the shoulder and use all but one of the pairs to work the half-stitch backing to the edge of the cloak.

5 Sew in seven pairs on the hand side of the sleeve and rib down the edge of the sleeve and up the back edge, back stitching to keep the rib flat while working around the curve. Sew out into the cloak.

6 Sew seven pairs into the back of the sleeve and use them to rib the scallops on the sleeve. Back stitch on each point to keep the rib flat. Turn at the top and work back in half stitch with the seven pairs. Carefully lay back the pairs at the tip of the sleeve.

7 Sew in seven pairs at the back of the sleeve and rib around the belt.

8 Fill in the body in whole stitch, starting at the bottom point. Sew in five pairs, hanging a coarse bobbin and one other with it to make a pair. Increase to 15 pairs at the widest point. Sew out into the cloak.

9 Sew seven pairs into the sleeve and rib along the edge of the tunic and along the bottom. Roll back and rib down the leg, along the top of the boot, up to the cloak and sew in to the sleeve; then use the same pairs for the other leg.

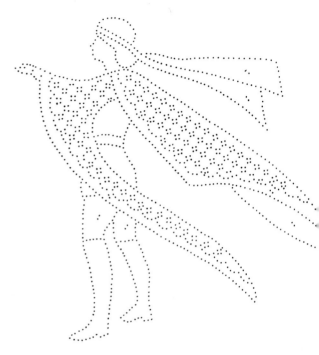

Pricking 38

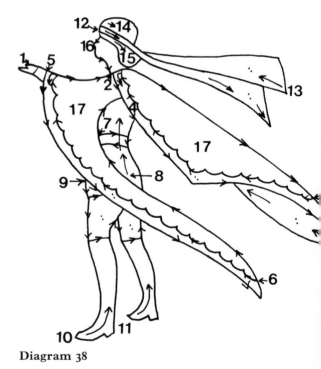

Diagram 38

82

Pattern 38 and 39 *Prince; princess*

10 Start at the tip of the left toe with six pairs and a coarse pair and work in whole stitch. Increase to ten pairs and the coarse pair at the ankle and add one more pair for the calf.

On reaching the ribbed section, cut out the coarse pair, change to half stitch and increase to 13 pairs at the widest part.

Change to whole stitch for the tunic and sew out into the sleeve.

11 Work the other leg in the same way.

12 Work the headband next. Start with five pairs and a coarse pair and work in half stitch. Continue on down the lower ribbon and increase to 11 pairs and the coarse pair at the widest part. Decrease and carefully lay back the ends at the tip of the ribbon.

13 Start at the bottom tip of the higher ribbon and sew out into the first one.

14 Work the top section of the hair in whole stitch, starting with six pairs and a coarse pair and increasing to nine pairs and the coarse pair. Sew out into the headband.

15 Now work the lower section of the hair, starting at the forehead with four pairs and a coarse pair and increasing to eight pairs and a coarse pair. Sew out into the ribbon.

16 Rib down the face with seven pairs.

17 The Four Pin filling is worked last of all.

39 *Princess* (120)

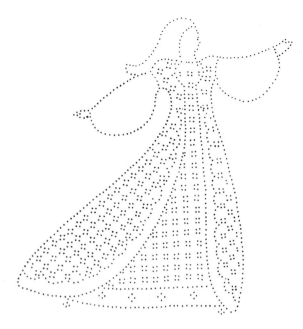

1 Start at the right-hand front edge of the cloak and work down in rib with the pinholes on the left. Rib down the inside edge, up the outside, around the armhole and across the neck, sewing into the start as it is worked over. Rib down the inside edge of the other side, up the outside edge, around the armhole, and along the top of the shoulder, and sew out into the neck. Leave the ends long as this will make sewing into the same place later much easier.

2 Sew seven pairs into the outside edge of the cloak and rib up the scallops. Back stitch at each point to enable the rib to lie flat. The pinhole side of the rib will be on the outside of the scallops. Use the same pairs to work the half stitch backing and sew out carefully at the bottom. Work the other side in the same way.

Diagram 39

3 Use 11 pairs and a coarse pair for the whole-stitch section, along the bottom of the dress, and sew out into the cloak. Work four pin buds where indicated on the pattern and make pearls along the bottom edge.

4 Sew in seven pairs and rib around the sleeves, starting at the armhole and finishing on the armhole. Use some of these pairs and some hung in along the armhole edge (ten in all), and fill in with half stitch. Increase to 14 pairs at the widest point.

Back stitch on the top side of the sleeve and finish at the wrist with six pairs. Use these to rib along the top of the hand and back to the wrist in whole stitch.

Both sleeves are worked in the same way.

5 Rib up the neck and the face, change to whole stitch and hang in a coarse pair and whole stitch down the hair. Lay back the ends carefully at the tip of the curl.

Pricking 39

Fillings
a Blossom (p.92)
b Four Pin (p.96)

40 *Girl with a parasol* (120)

Pattern 40   *Girl with a parasol (designed by Lee Ault and made by Tina Jackson)*

1 Rib around the central knot of the bow using six pairs. Sew into the starting pin without removing it and continue to rib around the bow (a). Use the rib pairs to fill in the central knot in whole stitch and continue the rib around the bow (b).

Sew in 14 pairs along the top of the bow (a) and work in whole stitch to fill in as far as the central knot when sewing, and finish off. Work bow (b) in the same way using 12 pairs.

2 Rib around the outside of the hat band and sew out the pairs into the top of the bow.

Sew in nine pairs along the top edge and fill in the band with whole stitch.

3 Rib down the back of the bonnet, using six pairs, and sew out into the bow. Fill in with half stitch by sewing in the pairs along the top edge, having 14 pairs at the widest part.

4 Make the front brim in the same way, using a maximum of 13 pairs when filling in with half stitch.

5 For the long ends of the bow start at both points with six pairs and a coarse pair. Work in whole stitch to where the two points meet. Join the two sections together, removing the centre coarse threads. Continue in whole stitch, decreasing as the lace narrows and sew out into the central knot.

6 Work in the same way as 5 and sewing out into 5 to finish.

7 Start the rib around the sleeve with six pairs under (b) and work in the direction indicated in the diagram, sewing out into bow (b). Sew in eight pairs along the top edge of the cuff and fill in with whole stitch. Work the Diamond filling.

Sew in 26 pairs along the cuff and fill in the sleeve with half stitch over the top of the filling.

8 Work the hand in the same way as the ends of the bow.

9 Work the handle of the parasol in whole stitch, carry the pairs across the back of the hand and change to rib for the stem.

10 Start at the bottom corner of the back section of the bodice with six pairs and a coarse pair, adding and decreasing as necessary.

11 Work in the same way as the previous section, dividing the pairs at the corner of the bow.

12 Sew six pairs into the back of the bodice and rib down the outside edge, along the bottom of the skirt and up the far edge to the sleeve.

Pricking 40

86

13 Work in rib from the bottom of the skirt to the bodice with the pinholes on the right.

14 Work the same as 13.

15 Work this and rib 16 in the same way but with the pinholes on the left.

17 Fill in the bottom of the skirt with whole stitch using 14 pairs. Sew in some of the pairs when passing over the ribbed sections and replace the pins in order to keep the pinholes distinct. Work the four pin buds in each section where indicated.

When sewing out these pairs at the skirt edge, each pair must be sewn using a raised sewing. Replace all the pins along the edge and bring the pairs back between the pins in their correct order. Tie each pair three times and cut them off. (The ends are now lying over the back of the lace.)

Make the Diamond filling in each section and back it with half stitch as follows: (c) 15 pairs; (d) 26 pairs; (e) 23 pairs; (f) 18 pairs; (g) 22 pairs.

18 Sew in six pairs at the bottom of the skirt and rib along the petticoat with a pearl edge.

19 Rib around both shoes to the top of the heel. Sew into the petticoat edge and use the same pairs to fill in the shoe with whole stitch.

20 Start at the point of the parasol and rib up the right-hand side of the centre section, down the left-hand side and along the bottom edge. (Sew into the starting point when passing, without removing the pin.)

Work to the back of the parasol, up the outside edge, down the front, along the bottom and sew out into the bonnet.

Next, rib up one of the remaining two sections and down the other.

21 Rib down the spike and use these pairs to fill in the central section with whole stitch, adding pairs as necessary and working the four pin buds as indicated.

The remaining four sections are worked by sewing in along the bottom edge of the parasol, working to the top and down an opposite section.

Diagram 40

four

HELPFUL HINTS

*Before starting a piece of lace wind the knot joining the two bobbins well on to one of them.

*To keep the pinholes small and neat on the edge, twist, put in the pin, make a whole stitch and pull up the pairs well. Twist both pairs three times and pull up well again, and also after the first stitch of the row.

*It is important that the pins slope slightly outwards and backwards.

*When adding new pairs, work the first row after the addition and pull the runners on the opposite side. This is the pair on which the new pair was added and will pull the edge of the lace into shape again. If you do not do this you often have a dip in the side of the lace.

*Always keep the bobbins the same length when working. Ideally this should be with 10cm (4in.) between the top of the bobbin and the lace.

*When finishing pairs from a rib into a rib, sew in the pairs and replace the pins. Lift all the pairs over the lace between the pins and then tie them three times and cut off.

*For the first piece of raised work, twisting four times instead of three for the pinholes helps to make the sewings easier.

*If in doubt as to whether to do a raised or flat sewing it is better to do a raised one.

*Use raised sewings for sewing out fillings so that the ends stay better over the back of the lace.

five

THE FILLINGS

1 Blossom

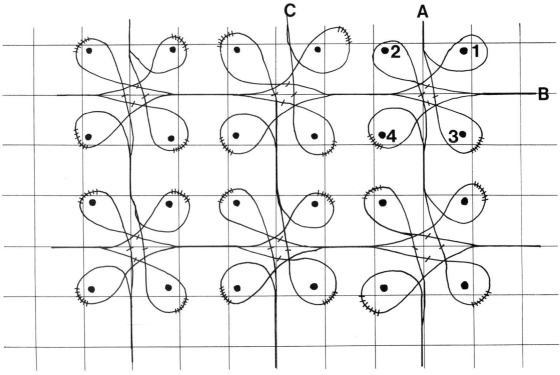

Filling 1   *Blossom*   1 square = 1mm

Sew two pairs at A and two pairs at B. With each of the two pairs, make a half stitch bar to reach to the group of four holes. These pairs are now numbered from left to right 1, 2, 3, and 4.

With pair 2 make right-hand pearl 1. Make a whole stitch with pairs 1 and 2.

Join the centre two pairs (2 and 3) with a whole stitch and twist them both once. Make a whole stitch with pairs 1 and 2.

With pair 1 make a left-handed pearl in hole 2. Make a whole stitch with pairs 1 and 2. Make a whole stitch with pairs 3 and 4.

Use pair number 4 to make right-handed pearl 3. Make a whole stitch with pairs 3 and 4. Twist pairs 2 and 3 once. Take pair 2 through pairs 3 and 4 in whole stitch.

Make the left-handed pearl 4 with pair 3. Make a whole stitch with pairs 3 and 4.

Make a half stitch bar with the two pairs hanging between holes 3 and 4 and leave them for the next row.

Make a half stitch bar with the pairs between holes 2 and 4 and also with the pairs hanging from C. These are now used for the next 'Blossom'.

2 Brick

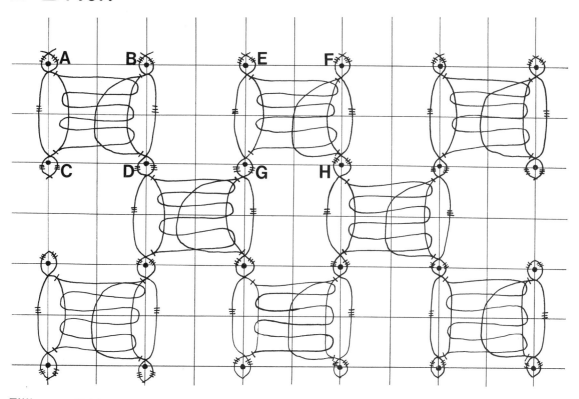

Filling 2   *Brick*

1 square = 1mm

Sew two pairs above each hole across the top of the pattern. Make a whole stitch and twist both pairs three times with each group, putting a pin between each of the two pairs. Enclose the pin with a whole stitch. Twist the left-hand pair from A and the right-hand pair from B three times. Twist the right-hand pair from A and the left-hand pair from B once. Use these pairs to make a leadwork, filling the space between the pins. Twist the pairs once. Work a whole stitch with the left-hand pair and the pair hanging from A, twist three times and put pin C between the pairs. Enclose the pin with a whole stitch. Work a whole stitch with the right-hand leadwork pair and the pair hanging from B, twist three times and put pin D between the pairs.

Enclose the pin with a whole stitch.

Repeat this with the pairs from E and F, etc. across the row. Twist the left-hand pair from D and the right-hand pair from G three times. Twist the right-hand pair from D and the left-hand pair from G once and use them to make the leadwork. Twist both pairs once at the bottom of the leadwork.

Make a whole stitch with the left-hand leadwork pair and the pair hanging from D, twist them three times and put a pin between them. Enclose the pin with a whole stitch.

Repeat this with the right hand leadwork pair and the pair from G. (The leadworks alternate on each row.)

93

3 Brick Variation

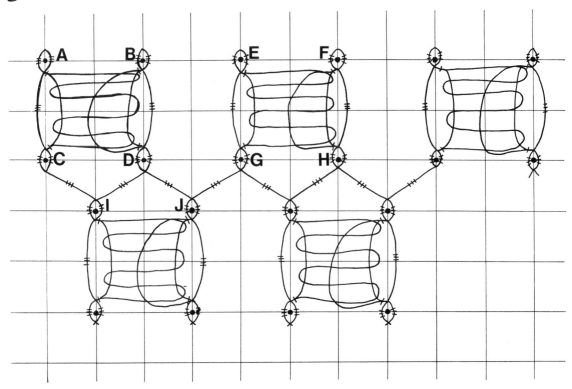

Filling 3   *Brick Variation*   1 square = 1mm

Copied from lace in the Royal Albert Memorial Museum, Exeter. Sew in two pairs above each hole of the filling.

With the two pairs from A make a whole stitch and twist both pairs three times. Put pin A between them. Enclose the pin with a whole stitch. Make a whole stitch with the two pairs from B, twist them three times and put the pin between them. Enclose the pin with a whole stitch.

Twist the left-hand pair from A and the right-hand pair from B three times. Twist the right-hand pair from A and the left-hand pair from B once, and make a leadwork with them to fill the space between the pinholes. Twist each pair once.

With the left-hand pair and the pair from A make a whole stitch. Twist both pairs three times and put pin C between them. Enclose the pin with a whole stitch and twist both pairs three times.

Take the right-hand leadwork pair and the pair from B and make a whole stitch. Twist both pairs three times and put pin D between them. Enclose the pin with a whole stitch and twist both pairs three times.

Repeat this with the pair from E and F. For the next row the pairs divide. The right-hand pair from C and the left-hand pair from D make a whole stitch, twist three times with both pairs and put pin I between them. Enclose the pin with a whole stitch.

Repeat with the pairs from D and G and put up pin J between them. This next block of brick is now worked the same as the first. (The filling makes diagonal lines of bricks.)

4 Diamond

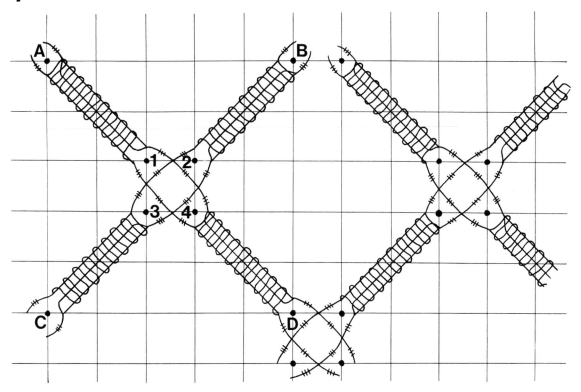

Filling 4   *Diamond*   1 square = 1mm

Sew a pair each side of a pinhole above A and B. Twist them three times and put a pin between them. With the pairs from A, make a leadwork to reach as far as hole 1. Twist three times and put a pin between them. Twist the pairs at B three times and put a pin between them. Make a leadwork to reach to hole 2, twist both pairs three times and put a pin between them.

Take the right-hand pair from 1 and the left-hand pair from 2 and make a whole stitch and three twists. (No pin.) Take the two left-hand pairs of the four and make a whole stitch and

three twists, and put a pin between them in hole 3. Make a whole stitch and three twists with the right-hand pairs, and put a pin between them in hole 4. Take the centre two pairs of the four and make a whole stitch and three twists. (No pin.) The left-hand two pairs now make a leadwork to reach to C. Twist both pairs three times and put a pin between them. The pairs from hole 4 make a leadwork to D, twist them three times and put a pin between them.

Each group is worked in this way.

95

5 *Four Pin*

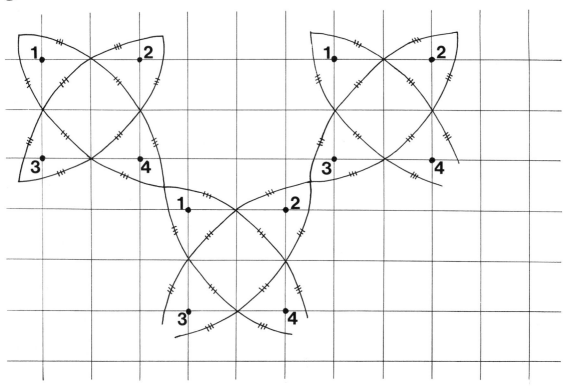

Filling 5   *Four Pin*   1 square = 1mm

Sew two pairs at an angle, above the top two holes of the pattern.

With the left-hand two pairs make a whole stitch, twist both pairs three times and put a pin between them in hole 1.

With the right-hand two pairs, make a whole stitch, twist both pairs three times and put a pin between them in hole 2.

Take the centre two pairs of the four, make a whole stitch and twist both pairs three times, but do not put in a pin.

Take the left-hand two pairs, make a whole stitch, twist both pairs three times and put a pin between them in hole 3.

Take the right-hand two pairs, make a whole stitch, twist both pairs three times and put a pin between them in hole 4.

Take the two centre pairs and make a whole stitch and twist both pairs three times but do not put in a pin. This completes the four holes.

The two pairs from 4 go to hole 1 to the right and the two pairs from 3 to hole 2 to the left.

6 Four Pin Flower and Leadwork

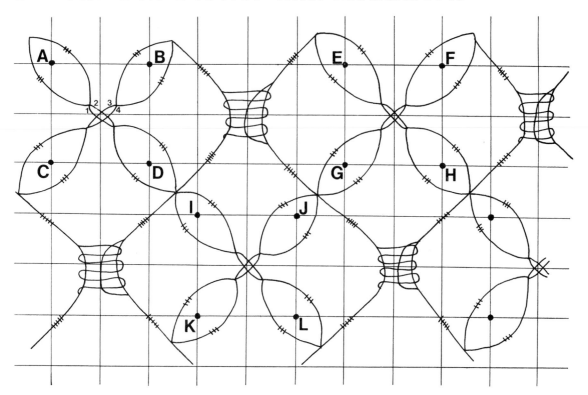

Filling 6   *Four Pin Flower and Leadwork*   1 square = 1mm

Copied from lace in Sidmouth Museum. Sew two pairs above hole A and three pairs above the other holes along the top of the filling.

Make a whole stitch and twist both pairs three times with the two pairs from A. Put the pin between them and enclose the pin with a whole stitch.

With the two left-hand pairs from B, make a whole stitch, twist them three times and put a pin between the pairs. Enclose the pin with a whole stitch.

Take pair 3 through 2 and 1 in whole stitch. Take pair 4 through pairs 2 and 1 in whole stitch. Make a whole stitch with the two left-hand pairs, twist them both three times and put pin C between them. Enclose the pin with a whole stitch.

Make a whole stitch with the two right-hand pairs, twist them both three times and put pin D

between them. Enclose the pin with a whole stitch.

Use the pair left at B and the left-hand pair from E to make a leadwork, first twisting both pairs five times. Twist both pairs five times again after the leadwork. Work the left-hand pair in whole stitch through the two pairs at D.

Next, work four pin flower EFGH in the same way as ABCD. Weave the right-hand leadwork pair through the two pairs at G. The two pairs at D now make a whole stitch and three twists, and pin I is put between them. The same is done with the two pairs from G for pin J. The rest of the four pin flower is completed in the same way as the first.

The leadworks and flowers alternate in each row. (If preferred a row of four pin flowers can be worked, before the leadworks between them are made.)

7 Four Pin Lattice

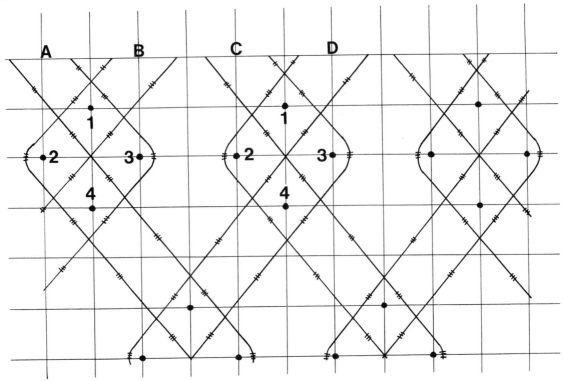

Filling 7   *Four Pin Lattice*   1 square = 1mm

Sew one pair into each side of pinholes A, B, C, D, etc. across the top of the lace. (These must be diagonally to right and left of the top pinholes of the fillings.) Twist all the pairs three times. Take the centre two pairs from A and B and make a whole stitch and three twists, and put pin 1 between them.

Take the left-hand two pairs and make a whole stitch and three twists, and put pin 2 between them. Take the right-hand two pairs and make a whole stitch and three twists, and put pin 3 between them. Make a whole stitch and three twists with the centre two pairs, and put pin 4 between them. Make a whole stitch and three twists with the left-hand pairs. (No pin.) Make a whole stitch and three twists with the right-hand pairs. (No pin.) Take the centre two pairs and make a whole stitch and three twists. (No pin.)

Repeat this with the pairs hanging from C and D, etc. across the row. The pairs now divide diagonally for the row beneath.

8 Italian

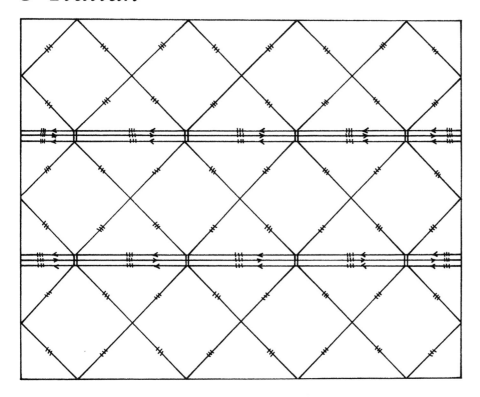

Filling 8 *Italian*

(No pricking is required for this filling.)

Sew two pairs into every hole, or every other hole, depending on how close the pinholes are to one another. Make a whole stitch with each group and twist both pairs three times. Sew out the extreme outside pairs, twist them both three times and leave them. Take one pair from each group, make a whole stitch and twist both pairs three times. Bring in the sewn pairs as these will now be needed. Make a whole stitch with the first sewn pair and the one next to it, but *do not twist*. Continue along the row making whole stitches but *do not twist*. (There should now be a row of diamonds.) Sew in one pair of runners on the right-hand side and twist them three times.

Make two whole stitches with the next two pairs and again twist the runner three times.

Continue in this way all across the row. After the last two whole stitches at the end of the row, twist the runners three times and sew them into the edge, in line with where they were sewn at the beginning of the row. Twist these same runners three times and make two whole stitches and three twists along the row as before. Again sew in the runners, twist them three times and work back to the left in the same way as before.

The next block of filling is worked in the same way as before, starting by using the groups of two pairs hanging together, and making the first whole stitch and three twists with them.

9 Leadworks and Lattice

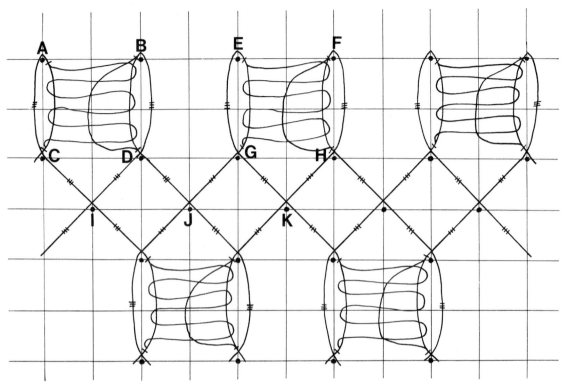

Filling 9   *Leadworks and Lattice*   1 square = 1mm

Sew in two pairs of bobbins above each hole in the row. Make a whole stitch with the pair hanging from A and B. Twist the left-hand pair from A and the right-hand pair from B three times.

Twist the right-hand pair from A and the left-hand pair from B once, and use them to make a square leadwork, to reach to C and D. Twist each pair once. Make a whole stitch with the pair left at A and the left-hand leadwork pair, and twist them both three times. Put pin C between the pairs. Make a whole stitch with the right hand leadwork pair and the pair left at B and twist them both three times. Put pin D between the pairs.

Make the holes E, F, G, and H, in the same way.

Take the right-hand pair from C and the left-hand pair from D, make a whole stitch and twist both pairs three times. Put pin I between them. Leave these two pairs and take the next two, make a whole stitch and three twists with both pairs and put pin J between them.

Continue all along the row. (The left hand pair from C and the last pair left at the end of the row will be sewn out into the edge of the lace.)

The two pairs hanging from J now work with the pairs to the left and right of them for the Leadwork pattern in the row below.

10 No Pin

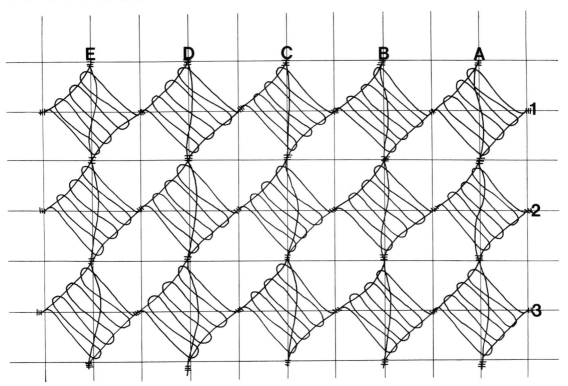

Filling 10 *No Pin*　　　　　　　　　　　　1 square = 1mm

(No pricking is required for this filling).

Sew one pair into every hole, or every alternate hole, depending on how far apart the holes are pricked along the edge of the lace. Twist each pair three times.

Sew pair 1, into the edge on the right-hand side and use to make the first leadwork. Twist both pairs three times. Take the runners and use the same bobbin to weave the next leadwork.

Repeat this all along the row, always using the same bobbin to weave the leadwork or they will not pull up at the end of the row. Having twisted the runners three times after the last leadwork, sew them into the hole opposite the hole into which they were sewn at the beginning of the row.

If the pairs are hung above each hole across the top of the pattern it is usually correct to sew the runner pairs one hole down on the side of the lace each time. If they are sewn into every other hole then the runners will usually need to be sewn into every other hole down the side of the lace.

For each row, a new pair of runners will have to be sewn in on the edge at the right-hand side.

11 *Pin and a Stitch*

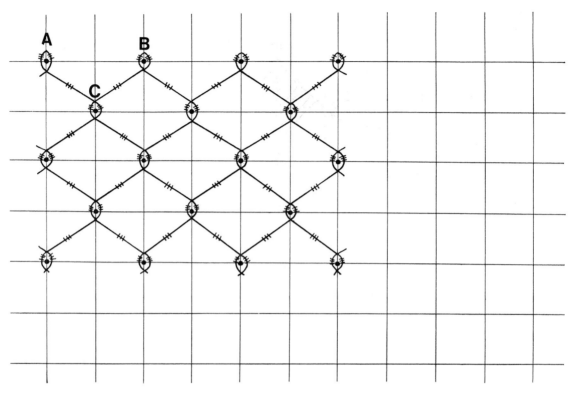

Filling 11 *Pin and a Stitch*

1 square = 1mm

Sew in two pairs above each hole along the filling.

With each two pairs make a whole stitch and twist three times. Put pin A between them. Enclose the pin with a whole stitch and twist both pairs three times. Repeat this along the row.

For the second row, take the right-hand pairs from A and the left-hand pair from B, make a whole stitch and twist both pairs three times. Put pin C between them and enclose it with a whole stitch and twist both pairs three times.

Leave these two pairs and, taking the next two, work them in the same way. (The pairs divide at the bottom of each pinhole and work to the left and right for the next hole).

12 Pin and a Stitch with Leadworks

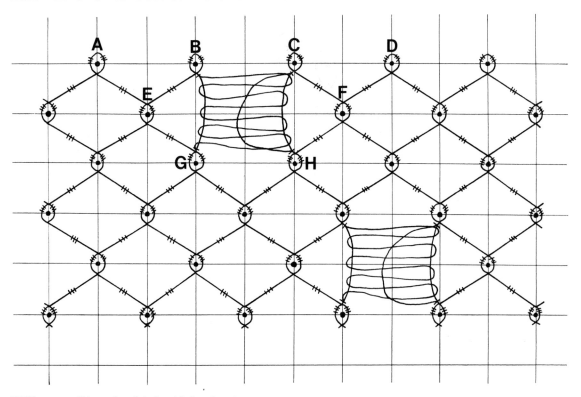

Filling 12 *Pin and a Stitch with Leadworks*   1 square = 1mm

The leadworks in this filling can be placed in various patterns either diagonally, alternate or in diamond patterns, etc. The main part of the filling is worked in the same way as for Pin and a Stitch.

With each of the two pairs above A, B, C, and D make a whole stitch and three twists, and put a pin between. Enclose the pins with a whole stitch. Twist all the pairs, except the ones working the leadwork, three times. Twist the right-hand pair from B and the left-hand pair from C once and use them to make a leadwork to fill the space between the pinholes BCGH. At the bottom of the leadwork twist each pair once.

Take the right-hand pair from E and the left-hand leadwork pair, make a whole stitch and twist both pairs three times. Put pin G between them, enclose it with a whole stitch and twist both pairs three times. Take the other leadwork pair and the left-hand pair from F and make a whole stitch and three twists. Put pin H between them, enclose the pin with a whole stitch and twist both pairs three times.

13 Six Pin Chain and Leadwork

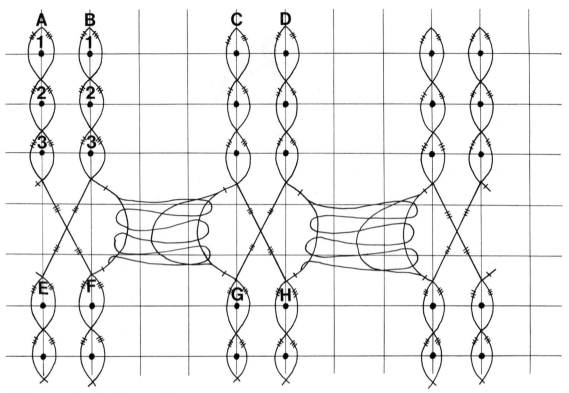

Filling 13 *Six Pin Chain and Leadwork*   1 square = 1mm

Copied from lace in Sidmouth Museum. Sew two pairs above each of the holes of the filling.

With the two pairs above A make a whole stitch, twist both pairs three times and put pin 1 between them. Make a whole stitch and three twists with the same pairs and put pin 2 between them. Repeat this for hole 3. Enclose the pin with a whole stitch.

Repeat this with the two pairs above B, C, and D etc. across the row.

Take the right-hand pair from below group A and the left hand pair from below group B. Twist them both three times, make a whole stitch and twist both three times again.

Take the right-hand pair from group B and the left-hand pair from group C. Twist them both once, make a small square leadwork and twist them both once again.

Make a whole stitch with the left-hand leadwork pair and the pair to their left. Twist both pairs three times and put pin 1 between them for the start of group F.

Sew in a pair of runners on the left-hand side to work with the pair from the cross at the bottom of groups A and B to make a whole stitch and three twists. Put pin 1 of group E between them.

All the groups are made in this way and are immediately beneath one another on each row.

14 *Straight Pin*

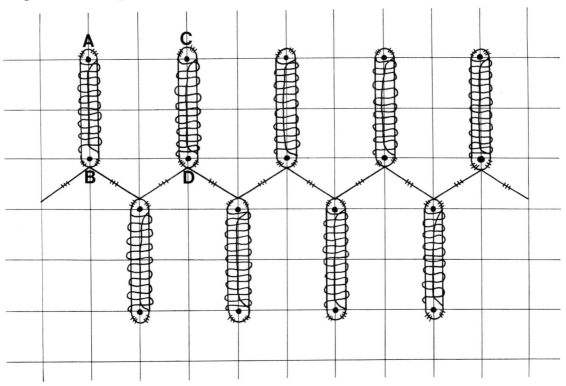

Filling 14   *Straight Pin*   1 square = 1mm

Sew two pairs above each hole across the top of the filling. With the first set of two pairs, make a whole stitch, twist the bobbins three times and put pin A between them. Use these pairs to make a narrow leadwork to reach to pin B. Twist the pairs three times and put pin B between them. Enclose the pin with a whole stitch and twist

both pairs three times. Repeat this with the pairs hanging above C, (and the rest of the row).

Take the right-hand pairs from B and the left-hand pairs from D and use these to continue the pattern in the row below. (The leadworks alternate on each row.)

15 Swing and a Pin

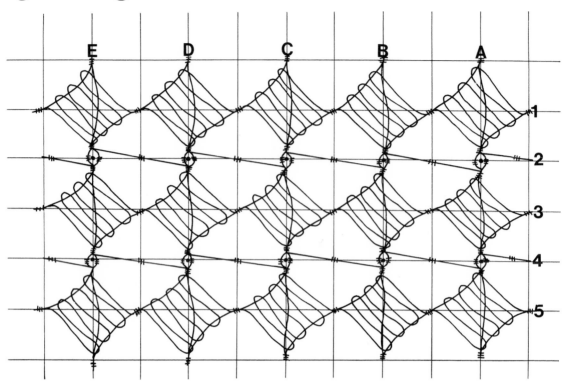

Filling 15 *Swing and a Pin*

1 square = 1mm

There is no pricking for this filling, it is pricked as it is worked.

Depending on how close the pinholes are sewn, one pair in every hole, or every other hole, across the top of the lace. Twist each pair three times.

Sew in a pair of runners (1), twist them three times and make a square leadwork with the pair hanging from A. Twist both pairs three times and then use the same runners for the remainder of the leadworks in the row. The same weaver must be used for each leadwork or they will not pull up at the end. Twist the runners three times and sew them out into the edge of the lace in line with where they were sewn in at the beginning of the row.

Sew in a pair of runners (2) and twist them three times. Make a whole stitch with the runners and the pair left at A. Twist them both three times and put a pin between them, below the bottom point of the leadwork. Enclose the pin with a whole stitch and twist both pairs three times. Leave the right-hand pair and continue to the next leadwork with the same runners. Twist three times at the end of the row and sew out into the lace.

These two rows complete the pattern.

16 *Swing and a Stitch*

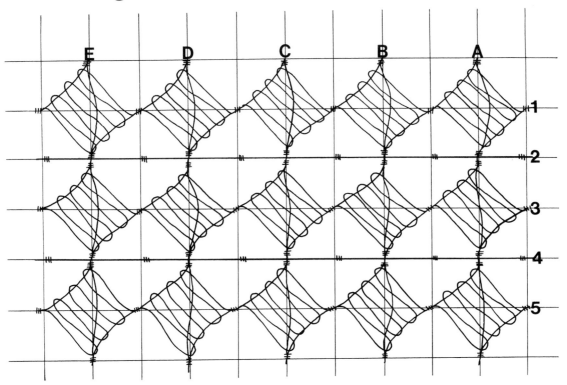

Filling 16   *Swing and a Stitch*   1 square = 1mm

(No pricking is needed for this filling.)

Sew one pair in every, or every other, hole across the top of the lace, depending how close the pinholes are. Twist them all three times.

Sew in a pair of runners (1), either in the next hole down on the right-hand side, or the next but one. Twist this pair three times and use it as the runners for the row of leadworks. Always use the same weaver for each leadwork or they will not pull up at the end of the row. Twist both pairs three times after each leadwork. Twist the runners three times at the end of the row and sew them out in a line with where they were sewn in at the beginning of the row.

Sew in a pair of runners (2) and twist them three times. Make a whole stitch with these and the pair hanging from the first leadwork. Twist both pairs three times. Continue likewise across the row. Again, sew the runners out in line with where they were sewn in at the beginning. (These two rows complete the pattern.)

17 Toad in the Hole

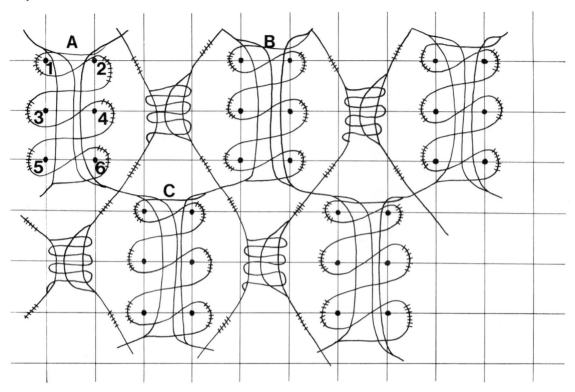

Filling 17 *Toad in the Hole*

1 square = 1mm

This filling is made in the same way as Whole Stitch Block, with the addition of leadworks between the snatches. An extra pair to right and left of the snatch will be required for the leadworks. With each of the two pairs above A, make a whole stitch and one twist. Work the far right hand pair in whole stitch through the others to the left, twist seven times and put in pin 1 under them.

The other holes are worked in the same way with the same pair as runners. After hole 6, twist seven times and work through to the left. Twist the two left-hand pairs once. Make a whole stitch and one twist with the pairs on the right. Twist the leadwork pairs five times and make a

square leadwork. Twist both five times after the leadwork.

The left-hand pair now works in whole stitch through the right-hand pairs from A and is twisted five times ready for the next leadwork. Next, work snatch B in the same way as snatch A.

Work the pair left hanging from the first leadwork through the pairs on the left of snatch B and twist it five times. The right-hand pairs from A and the left-hand pairs from B are now ready to work snatch C. (If preferred all the snatches in the row can be worked first and then the leadwork.)

108

18 Toad in the Hole with Enclosed Pins

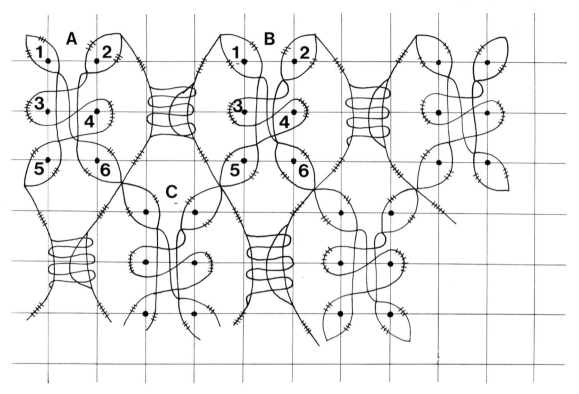

Filling 18 *Toad in the Hole with Enclosed Pins*   1 square = 1mm

(This filling was taught to us by Christine Hawken.)

Sew in three pairs diagonally above each hole, except the first one, where only two pairs are needed. With the left-hand pairs from A, make a whole stitch, twist both pairs three times and put pin 1 between them. Enclose the pin with a whole stitch. Make a whole stitch with the two left-hand pairs above hole 2. Twist them both three times and put pin 2 between them. Enclose the pin with a whole stitch. The far right-hand pair of the four now works in whole stitch through the three pairs to the left. Twist the bobbins seven times and put pin 3 under them. Work back to the right in whole stitch and twist seven times. Put pin 4 under the pair and again work through to the left. Take the two left-hand pairs, make a whole stitch and twist both pairs three times. Put pin 5 between them and enclose the pin with a whole stitch. Take the two right-hand pairs and make a whole stitch. Twist both pairs three times, put pin 6 between them and enclose it with a whole stitch. The pair left hanging above the hole 2 of snatch A and the left-hand pair from snatch B are now used for the leadwork. Twist both pairs five times, make a small, square leadwork and again twist both pairs five times. The left-hand pair now works in whole stitch through the pairs at hole 6 of the first snatch. If desired, all the snatches in a row can be worked first and then the leadworks.

109

19 Toad in the Hole with Wide Leadworks

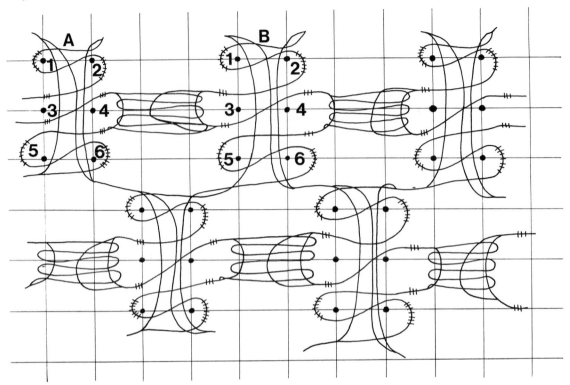

Filling 19 *Toad in the Hole with Wide Leadworks* 1 square = 1mm

Sew in two pairs at an angle above each of the holes of the filling.

With each group, make a whole stitch and twist both pairs once. Take the right-hand pair from group A and work it in whole stitch through the other three pairs. Twist seven times and put pin 1 under them. Work the same pair in whole stitch to the right through the three pairs, twist seven times and put pin 2 under them. Work in whole stitch through the three pairs to the left and twist three times and put pin 3 under them. Work in the same way with group B, etc.

If group A is near the edge of the lace, sew in the weaver pair left at 3, sew again one hole lower down and twist three times. Work in whole stitch to the right through the three pairs, twist three times and put up pin 4 under them. Use this pair left at 3 from group B to make a leadwork to fill the space between the pinholes and twist both pairs three times. Take the left-hand pair from the leadwork and work in whole stitch to the left through three pairs, twist seven times and put pin 5 under them. Work in whole stitch to the right through the three pairs, twist seven times and put pin 6 under them. Work in whole stitch to the left and twist the last two pairs once. Take the right-hand two pairs, make a whole stitch and twist both pairs once. The right-hand pair left from the leadwork are now worked to the right through three pairs, where they are twisted three times and pin 4 put under them. The leadwork is now made with the pair from the next snatch, the group B is now finished in the same way as A.

At the bottom of each row the pairs divide diagonally for the next row.

20 *Toad in the Hole Variation*

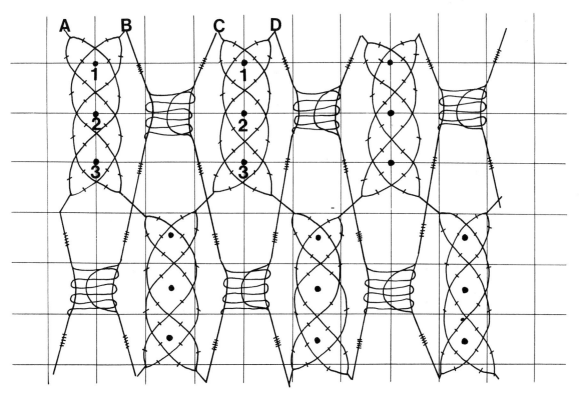

Filling 20 *Toad in the Hole Variation*   1 square = 1mm

Sew two pairs diagonally above each set of holes across the pattern. One extra pair will be needed to the right and the left of the groups of holes for the leadworks.

With each of the two pairs above A make a half stitch bar of three half stitches. Do the same with the left-hand two pairs at B. Make a whole stitch and one twist with the two centre pairs of the four, and put pin 1 between them. Make a whole stitch and one twist with the two left-hand pairs. (No pin.) Make a whole stitch and one twist with the two right-hand pairs. (No pin.) Take the centre two pairs and make a whole stitch and one twist, and put pin 2 between them. Make a whole stitch and one twist with the two left-hand pairs. (No pin.). Make a whole stitch and one twist with the two right-hand pairs. (No pin.) Take the centre two pairs and make a whole

stitch and one twist and put pin 3 between them. Make a whole stitch and one twist with the two left-hand pairs. (No pin.) Make a whole stitch and one twist with the two right hand pairs. (No pin.) Take the centre two pairs and make a whole stitch and one twist to enclose the last pin. Work a bar of three half stitches with the two left-hand pairs and then the two right-hand pairs.

Work block CD in the same way. Twist the remaining pair at B and C five times and use them to work a small square leadwork. Twist the pairs both five times and work the left-hand pair in whole stitch through the right-hand bar of the previous block. Work the right-hand leadwork pair through the left-hand bar of the second block in whole stitch.

The pairs now work diagonally to the block below.

21 Trolly Net

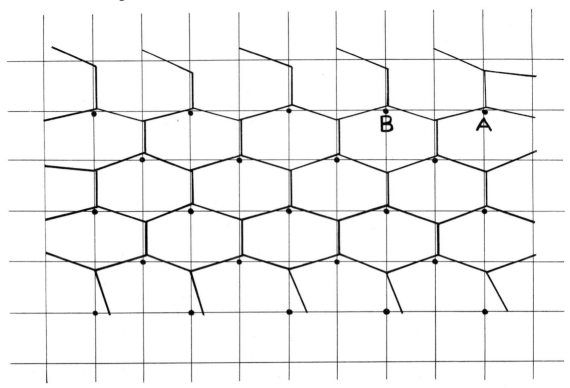

Filling 21 *Trolley Net*   1 square = 1mm

Sew in one pair between and above the first row of holes in the filling. Sew in one pair on the right as runners and twist all the pairs two or three times. Take the pair to the right of hole A and the runners and make a half stitch and *four* twists. Put a pin between the pairs. Leave the right-hand pair, and take the left-hand pair and the pair hanging to the right of hole B to make the next half stitch and *four* twists for the next pinhole. Continue in the same way for the rest of the row. Sew out the runners. Sew in another pair of runners on the right-hand side for the next row and twist them three times.

Work each row in the same way.

When using 120 thread, the net can be made by only twisting *twice* instead of four times after each half stitch.

22 Whole Stitch Block

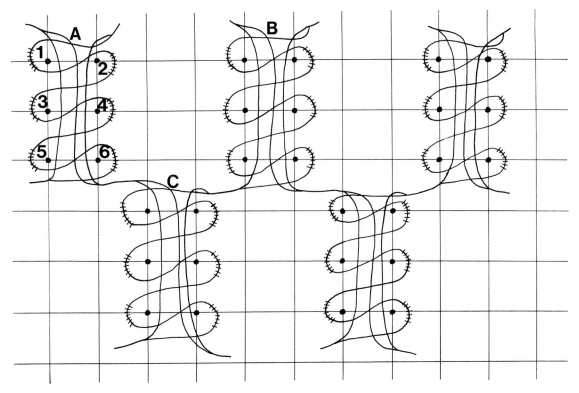

Filling 22 *Whole Stitch Block*

I square = Imm

Sew two pairs diagonally above each hole in the row.

Take each of the pairs above group A and make a whole stitch and one twist. Work the far right-hand pair through the three to the left in whole stitch, twist seven times and put in pin 1 under them. Work to and fro in this way with the same pair until hole 6 has been reached.

After putting in this pin and twisting seven times, work through to the left. Twist the two left-hand pairs once. Make a whole stitch with the two right-hand pairs and twist them both once.

Work snatch B in the same way.

For the next row the right-hand pairs from A and the left-hand pairs from B make snatch C.

23 Whole Stitch Block Variation

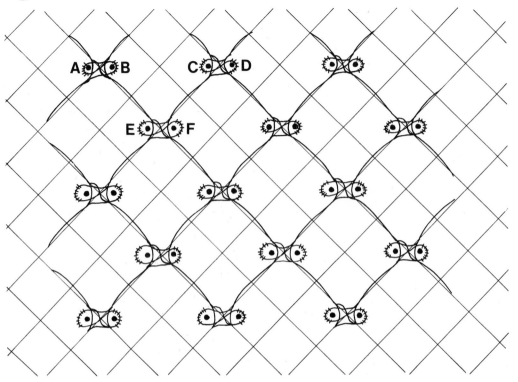

Filling 23 *Whole Stitch Block Variation*

1 square = 1mm

Sew two pairs diagonally above each two holes of the pattern along the top row.

With each two pairs make a half stitch plait to reach above the first two holes. Take the second pair from the right through the two pairs to the left in whole stitch. Twist seven times and put pin A under them. Work in whole stitch with the same pair through the three pairs to the right. Twist seven times and put pin B under them. Work in whole stitch through two pairs to the left and leave the runners

Repeat this with the other sets of four pairs across the row. (The pair left at A will be worked in half stitch plait and sewn out diagonally into the edge of the lace.)

Take the two pairs from B and make a half stitch plait to reach above hole E. Take the two left-hand pairs from C and make a half stitch plait with them to reach above F. Take the second pair from the right and weave through to the left in whole stitch as for AB.

Bibliography

Devonia, *The Honiton Lace Book*, (The Bazaar Office, London, first published 1873; reprinted by Paul Minet, London, 1972)

Luxton, Elsie, *The Technique of Honiton Lace*, (B.T. Batsford Ltd, London, First published 1979)

Luxton, Elsie, *Honiton Lace Patterns*, (B.T. Batsford Ltd, London, 1983)

Maidment, Margaret, *A Manual of Hand-Made Bobbin Lace*, (Charles T Branford Co, Boston, 1954; reprinted by Piccadilly Rare Books, Paul Minet, London)

Palliser, *The History of Lace*, (E. P. Publishing Ltd, first published 1902)

Penderel Moody, A., *Devon Pillow Lace*, (Cassell & Co Ltd, first published 1907)

Treadwin, *Antique Point and Honiton Lace*, (Ward Lock & Tyler, London, first published 1874)

List of suppliers

Honiton bobbins and threads

The Honiton Lace Shop
44 High Street
Honiton
Devon

DJ Hornsby
149 High Street
Burton Latimer
Kettering
Northants NN15 5RL
and
25 Manwood Avenue
Canterbury
Kent CT2 7AH

Tim Parker
124 Corhampton Road
Boscombe East
Bournemouth
Dorset BH6 5NZ

George White
Delaheys
Thistle Hill
Knaresborough
North Yorkshire HG5 8LS

Bobbins only

Bryn Phillips
'Pantaglas'
Cellan
Lampeter
Dyfed SA48 8JD

Bucks Bobbins
Woodside
Greenlands Lane
Prestwood
Gt Missenden
Bucks HP16 9QU

Christine and David Springett
21 Hillmorton Road
Rugby
Warwickshire CV22 5DF

Frames and mounts for lace

Doreen Campbell
Highcliff
Bremilham Road
Malmesbury
Wiltshire SN16 0OQ

Index